Greece and the Eurozone Crisis: What is to be done?

A Pamphlet

Greece and the Eurozone Crisis: What is to be done?

A Pamphlet

Karl Heinz Roth

Winchester, UK
Washington, USA

First published by Zero Books, 2013
Zero Books is an imprint of John Hunt Publishing Ltd., Laurel House, Station Approach,
Alresford, Hants, SO24 9JH, UK
office1@jhpbooks.net
www.johnhuntpublishing.com
www.zero-books.net

For distributor details and how to order please visit the 'Ordering' section on our website.

ISBN: 978 1 78099 824 4

A CIP catalogue record for this book is available from the British Library.

Design: Stuart Davies

Printed and bound by CPI Group (UK) Ltd, Croydon, CR0 4YY

CONTENTS

Ὕβριν χρή σβεννύναι μάλλον ή πυρκαϊήν (ancient Greek) /
Περισσότερο κι απ' την πυρκαγιά πρέπει κανείς να
κατασβήνει την έπαρση (modern Greek)
Hubris needs putting out, even more than a house on fire.
(Heraclitus)

Γι' αυτά αγωνιστήκαμε. Δεν τα πουλάμε
This [the cultural heritage of antiquity] is what we have fought
for – it is not for sale.
(General Makryjannis, revolutionary and Greek freedom fighter,
1821)

OXI – No!
(Greek response to the Italian ultimatum of 28 October 1940)

Θάνατος στο Φασισμό – death to fascism!
(Slogan of the Greek resistance against the German occupation,
1941–1944)

Κάτω η Χούντα! Ψωμί, Παιδεία, Ελευθερία!
Down with the junta! Bread, education, liberty!
(Slogan of the students in Athens protesting the military
dictatorship, 1973)

Πριν από εβδομήντα χρόνια πολεμήσαμε γενναία ενάντια στα
γερμανικά τάνκς
και τα αεροπλάνα. Τώρα έρχονται ξανά οι Γερμανοί
γραβατομένοι. Τα έχομε
χαμένα
Seventy years ago, we fought bravely against German tanks and
planes. Now the Germans are arriving in suits and ties – and we
don't know what to do.
(Remark by an elderly Greek man, made during a conversation
with the author in a *kaphenion* in the city of Ioannina, April 2011)

Before the Greek Debt Crisis

In the spring of 2012, the euro crisis intensified dramatically. The epicenter of the crisis is Greece, a country that has been experiencing a severe recession since the beginning of the world economic crisis. What outcome this recession will yield is a decisive question not just for Greece, but for all of Europe and indeed for the entire world economy. We need therefore to consider the story behind this crisis, and the restructuring programs imposed, since May of 2010, by the so-called "troika" (the European Commission, the European Central Bank and the International Monetary Fund). We also need to consider possible alternatives to these restructuring programs.

In 1981, Greece became a member of the European Community. A spirit of optimism prevailed in the country. The Socialist Party (PASOK), an offshoot of the Pan-Hellenic Resistance Movement against the 1967–1974 military dictatorship, had won the parliamentary elections for the first time. Due to its welfare-oriented platform, PASOK enjoyed widespread popular support.

As the conservative Karamanlis government stepped down, there began an era of social, cultural, scholarly and economic progress. This trend was in no way affected by the monetary restrictions associated with the European Monetary System that had been introduced within the European Community in 1979.[1] Greece was not to join this system until 1993. Like the currencies of the other new southern European member states (Portugal and Spain), the drachma was kept outside the currency agreement. While the intra-European disparities in economic development entailed certain distortions of competition, the Greek government was able to compensate for their effects by periodically devaluing the Greek currency. Thus there was little pressure to reconfigure Greek economic policy on the model of the European Community's core states. Between 1979 and 1992, the drachma was depreciated by 86 percent. In this way, the prices of Greek exports to the European Community's core states were lowered almost by half. Conversely, the prices of West German and French exports to Greece were increased almost by half.

This monetary and economic approach, favorable to Greece and the other countries of the European periphery, became unviable in 1992. Responding to the pressures engendered by the crisis-ridden development of their own national economies, the governments of the European Community's core states imposed a new framework, which has gone down in the annals of economic history as the Maastricht Treaty. It was designed to establish the contractual foundations of the European Community's transition to the European Union. The so-called convergence criteria at the core of the Treaty established parameters for inflation, national budgets, exchange rates and interest rates. They also introduced a cap on annual debt (three percent of the gross national product or GDP), thereby setting the course for the introduction of a single currency, the euro.

PASOK had been re-elected as the governing party in 1993. Its economic decision-makers and planners now found themselves in a squeeze. For Greece as for other countries, implementation of the Maastricht standards entailed abandonment of a policy of full employment that had until then been bolstered by a robust welfare state. The Greek government was forced to begin working towards the flexibilisation of employment relations and the deregulation of the public sector. Officially, it played along and made an effort to improve the public sector's economic efficiency. But due to pressure exerted by Greece's strong union movement, effective deregulation and the lowering of mass incomes were out of the question. It was only in 1996, when the neoliberal Kostas Simitis replaced the deceased Andreas Papandreou as head of government and curbed the influence of

PASOK's previously dominant party left, that the consensus on the welfare state was significantly challenged. If the floodgates were still not opened all the way, this was because there emerged within parliament a stable left-wing opposition that acted in concert with the traditionally influential communist bloc at critical moments. Major strikes and social struggles limited the extent of the welfare and wage cuts. However, Greece's competitiveness on the European market declined continuously. As a result, the country went from a positive to a negative trade balance and its budget deficit soared. Even prior to the late 1990s, the budget deficit's annual increase exceeded five percent of GDP, and total debt soon exceeded annual economic growth. These were blatant violations of the criteria stipulated in the Maastricht Treaty, and so the emergent scenario of over-indebtedness was veiled by means of statistical manipulations. By the late 1990s, Greek policy was significantly out of step with the process of neoliberal restructuring that countries such as England, France and Italy had been undergoing since the 1980s, and which was also increasingly evident in Germany and the Low Countries.

Nonetheless, in 2001, Greece was admitted to the eurozone, which had in the meantime been established within the European Union. While it is true the basic statistical data Athens provided to Brussels concealed the extent of Greece's economic imbalances, everyone involved was aware that Greece did not satisfy the criteria stipulated in the Maastricht Treaty, particularly the Treaty's budgetary parameters.[2] Why the course was nevertheless set for Greece's admission to the eurozone is something we will only know with certainty when the relevant documents are made public. Yet we can safely assume, even today, that geostrategic and short-term political goals played a decisive role. Two years after the destruction of Yugoslavia, Greece was a crucial outpost from which to begin integrating the Balkan states into the EU. It also secured the southeastern flank of the EU's planned "eastward enlargement." But short-term political goals also played an important role. The Greek Supreme Court had just accepted compensation claims by victims of the German occupation of Greece, and it had declared the confiscation of German assets legal.[3] No one but the Greek government could halt the proceedings. It did so after the German government promised to support Greece's application for eurozone membership.

From the perspective of the Greek elites at the time, admission to the eurozone was attractive. They were able to instantly abandon their extremely depreciated currency and exchange it for the "hard" euro, which presented them with extremely cheap refinancing options. There followed a period of rapid economic growth, with annual growth rates of between 3.7 and 5.2 percent; this period lasted until 2007. Maritime logistics, the petroleum-processing industry, tourism, construction and banking all flourished. To this were added massive imports of French, German and Swiss capital and ample European Commission subsidies for the development of infrastructure; given Greece's heightened geostrategic importance, these were considered a safe long-term investment. No one who remembers the Greece of the last century can fail to be struck by the tremendous amount of infrastructural investment the country has seen since then: witness the north-south highway from Thessaloniki to Athens, the west-east highway from the Ionian Sea to the Turkish border in western Thrace (especially important in military terms), the suspension bridge near Patras, which connects the Peloponnese with western Greece, Athens International Airport, the Attica ring road, the Athens subway, the Piraeus container port and the new suburban railways in Athens. To this were added the vast construction projects associated with the 2004 Olympics, which carried the real estate boom to extremes.

In parallel with this, Greece indulged in exuberant military spending. Between 1992 and 2008, the country imported 75 billion euros worth of military equipment, mainly frigates from France and tanks and submarines from Germany. Annual military expenditure rose to 4.3 percent of GDP, more than twice the corresponding figure for Germany. This ramp-up was legimitated by reference to Greece's "hereditary enemy" Turkey – a NATO member like Greece itself. Turkey had conquered and annexed part of Cyprus in 1974, and its military expenditure was even higher than that of Greece during this period. German and French defense contractors were the laughing third party and the profiteers of this regional conflict. At the outbreak of the current world economic crisis, the two antagonists in the eastern Mediterranean were the foremost recipients of German arms exports: Turkey headed the list with 15.2 percent, followed by Greece with 12.9 percent.[4]

The profiteers of the short-lived euro boom are easily identified. In essence, three closely interconnected sections of the ruling elite divided the spoils between themselves. First and foremost, there were the family clans who own the lion's share of Greece's shipping and banking capital, as well as most of its petrochemical industry. During the Simitis era, the business taxes to be paid by them were lowered to 25 percent, allowing them to enrich themselves dramatically during the economic boom. The more liquidity they disposed of, the less inclined they were to pay taxes at all. This led to a remarkable deterioration in the tax compliance of parts of the conservative upper middle class (doctors, real estate brokers, high-ranking bank employees, lawyers). Prior to the outbreak of the world economic crisis, the country's top 30,000 families held more than 250 billion euros in capital assets. Of these, 100 billion alone were held as bank deposits; at least another 100 billion were transferred abroad.

The second group was represented by people from Europe's leading capital goods, construction and armament corporations, as well from the European financial sector. These segments of European capital have traditionally enjoyed close ties with the families controlling Greece's shipping and banking capital. For example, the Latsis clan, which domiciles in Switzerland, is bound up with Deutsche Bank AG and Switzerland's two major banks; ThyssenKrupp is bound up with the Greek shipbuilding industry; Germany's and France's leading construction companies are bound up with the Greek real estate sector; the French and Franco-Belgian banks Société Générale, Crédit Agricole and Dexia control significant parts of the Greek financial sector, via their holding companies and subsidiary companies. It was by way of these ties that the past decade's major investments in infrastructure were planned and implemented; responsibility for refinancing and hedging the investments lay with the treasury. It was only after the infrastructure boom that the issuing of two-, five- and ten-year government bonds outstripped the analogous lending practices of the eurozone's other peripheral states.

The third profiteer of the euro boom was the political class of Greece, represented, since the end of the military dictatorship, by the two major parties PASOK and Nea Dimokratia (ND). Following the economic paradigm shift imposed by Kostas Simitis in 1996 and the elimination of the party left, PASOK's reservations about the major entrepreneurial dynasties, the orthodox state church and the military-industrial complex were dropped. PASOK also entered into an unqualified symbiosis with the ruling elites, especially with regard to infrastructural investment, defense contracts and the refinancing guarantees these inevitably entailed. During the boom period, Siemens alone mobilized some 15 million euros in slush money with an eye to gaining control of the Greek telecommunications provider OTE,[5] influencing the Defense Ministry's contracting activities and securing for itself the most important of the investment projects associated with the Olympics.[6] But that was only the tip of the iceberg. The European investors' onetime deposits on the bank accounts of PASOK's and ND's leading politicians merely supplemented long-term bank loans. The two parties used these loans both to maintain their apparatus of functionaries and to finance electoral campaigns. The systematic purchase of the country's politicians and their associated apparatuses of power and propaganda became an integral component of the boom period.

Thus when PASOK lost the elections in 2004 and the ND candidate Kostas Karamanlis became head of government, this was a mere change of label, entailing no more than a shift in the spectrum of favored social groups. As a result of this sort of clientelism, corruption and greed spread through broad strata of society. It is appropriate to speak of a system of social corruption that stalls the development of solidarity and social equality so urgently required today.

The ruling classes' unbridled *enrichez vous* already had a serious downside prior to the outbreak of the crisis. At the beginning of the new millennium, Greece developed a consistently negative trade balance. The budget deficit got seriously out of hand, due to the refinancing costs associated with the country's infrastructural investments. There began a creeping process of deindustrialization, as the country's relatively high unit labor costs and its continuously declining competitiveness could no longer be compensated for by devaluing the national currency. Greek exports within the EU declined correspondingly. The option of reorienting Greek export policy towards developing and newly industrializing countries was also increasingly unviable, as these countries had themselves become export-oriented low-wage countries that were out-competing Greek products and services. Thus the loss of national sovereignty in the field of monetary policy not only eliminated the compensatory levers of "external" devaluation it also confronted the Greek economy with a "squeeze" situation with regard to trade policy. Greece faced the prospect of being crushed between the export pressures emanating from the core states of the EU, states whose economies are characterized by a high degree of technological development and an advanced organization of production, and the trade offensive begun by the low-wage countries of the global periphery. Unemployment rose markedly. Young high school and university graduates who did not yet dispose of any employment guarantees were especially affected. They were increasingly forced to fall back on the socially unprotected, temporary and poorly paid employment relations that had emerged in the wake of the illegal immigration of the 1990s, leading to the rise of a veritable shadow economy. This development, unheard of in Greece, was increasingly interpreted as a worrisome portent by social science scholars; there was talk of the development of a new "700-euro generation." The term was quickly appropriated as an identity-establishing self-description by the emergent social movements of young precarious workers and illegal immigrants.

In the Vortex of the World Economic Crisis

In the course of 2008, the shock waves emanating from the world economic crisis reached Greece. Maritime logistics collapsed and the shipping companies, retailers and port operators active in this industry lost more than a fourth of their revenue. To this was added a drastic downturn in the tourism sector: in 2008 and 2009, the number of vacationers visiting Greece declined by about 20 percent. These effects were directly passed on to Greek banks. Like those of other countries, the Greek financial sector needed to be sustained by state guarantees in the spring of 2009. The contraction of the Greek economy's key sectors had far-reaching structural consequences. Since primary and secondary market exports declined equally, the process of deindustrialization was accelerated. Unemployment climbed above the 10-percent mark, and only two thirds of new first-time job seekers could still expect to find employment, a marked deterioration of job entry conditions notwithstanding. This affected mass consumption. The Greek economy went on to lose its domestic buttress as well, entering a recession that persists to this day and has worsened continuously. While the decline in annual economic output remained at just under 5 percent of GDP until 2010, this margin was significantly exceeded the following year.

Rescue operations to bolster the financial sector, declining fiscal revenue and rapidly rising social expenditure further increased the public debt. The full extent of the economic imbalances became apparent for the first time in late 2009, when the PASOK leadership – it had in the meantime been voted back into government – faced growing pressure from the EU and was no longer able to present whitewashed statistics. Little by little, corrected data were published, revealing that the annual budget deficit had gone from 9.8 percent of GDP in 2008 to 15.4 percent in 2009.[7] While new debt declined to 10.5 percent the following year, total debt soared, unchecked, from roughly 111 percent of GDP in 2008 to 127 percent and then 148 percent in 2009 and 2010, respectively. By 2010, Greece was in debt to the tune of 340 billion euros. The interest and amortization payments accruing on this debt were projected to reach an aggregate volume of at least 150 billion euros by 2015. Since the economic situation continued to deteriorate, ruling out a rapid return to sufficient levels of growth, it was already clear in early 2010 that the only way to stabilize the Greek economy was by means of a radical debt cut, with creditors waiving at least three quarters of their claims.

The response by international and European creditors was correspondingly drastic. In particular, the boards of Europe's major banks tried to get rid of their Greek bond packages as quickly as possible, despite insurance companies raising risk premiums continuously.[8] From the spring of 2010, this process went through several stages; in the end, it was increasingly reminiscent of the proverbial race between the hare and the hedgehog. On the free bond markets, the interest on Greece's two-year bonds repeatedly increased to as much as 40 percent. Rising risk premiums pushed the interest on ten-year bonds as high as 16 percent at ever shorter intervals. Under these circumstances, there was no longer any way of refinancing Greek public debt on the free bond markets. If they did not want to throw in the towel and proclaim national bankruptcy, the political classes of Greece and the eurozone needed to begin searching for an alternative. Since the Papandreou government no longer disposed of any sovereignty in the field of monetary policy, certain options were no longer available: in particular, that of inconspicuously lightening the debt burden by means of hyperinflation and that of combining inflation with a debt moratorium, in preparation for an international arbitration process by which to shift the bulk of the burden to creditors. It would nevertheless have been possible, even in early 2010, to opt for a sovereign default, thereby forcing the hand of the EU's decision-making bodies and enforcing a radical debt cut. But PASOK's earlier embrace of market radicalism had eliminated the conceptual foundations of such an approach. PASOK also lacked the political will to confront the monetary union's decision-making bodies, not to mention the stamina that a sovereign default would have required. Jorgos Papandreou and his staff chose to eat humble pie and bow down before the European Commission, the European Central Bank and the decision-making centers of the eurozone. Since the euro bloc's policymakers opted to bring in the International Monetary Fund (IMF), May 2010 saw the establishment of a *de facto* forced administration, soon to be known as the "troika."

Greece Under De Facto Forced Administration

In early May of 2010, the EU's decision-making bodies and the IMF provided Greece with funds to allow it to service its public debt without recourse to the free capital markets. In return, the PASOK government agreed to reduce its budget deficit by means of a comprehensive "internal depreciation." Of the total of 110 billion euros, the EU bodies provided 80 billion, and the IMF 30 billion. Interestingly, the interest charged was only marginally lower than the interest rates on the capital markets (5 percent on average). Thus the thumbscrews were applied. Under these circumstances, the sums to be paid in the years to come could only be mobilized by rapidly implementing significant wage, income and price reductions, in combination with major social cuts and drastic tax hikes. The austerity program was intended to siphon 30 billion euros out of the Greek economy within three years; cost reductions and additional revenue were to increase the government budget by this sum, so that it could then be used to service debt and interest. The Greek legislative machine got to work and pushed the agreement through parliament. It did so in flagrant violation of elementary principles of constitutional law. Taxes on consumption (so-called sales tax) were raised to 23 percent. Public sector employees were forced to accept wage cuts as high as 30 percent; to this were added increases in wage and personal income tax.

The agreement caused some controversy within the decision-making bodies of the eurozone and the EU, since it merely seemed to postpone a national bankruptcy that appeared inevitable in the long run, at the cost of significantly increasing the risk of default. Franco-German defense contractors were particularly keen on the agreement being ratified; in return for the loan, they were provided with guarantees that previously rescinded contracts concerning the purchase of 3 billion euros worth of military vessels, submarines and tanks would be honored after all. Even more was at stake for the major banks: their managers had calculated that deferral of national bankruptcy by at least one to two years was decisive for their survival. At the time of the agreement, Greek financial institutions held Greek bonds worth more than 40 billion euros. Even a debt cut based on the market value of Greek bonds (60 percent of par value) would have resulted in the immediate bankruptcy of these financial institutions. The situation was no less critical for the French, Swiss and German financial corporations active in Greece. By the spring of 2010, Greek foreign debt had risen to about 210 billion euros (about 300 billion US dollars). Almost two thirds of this debt was owed to French, Swiss and German credit institutions; their shares of the total claims were estimated at 25 percent (France), 21 percent (Switzerland) and 14.3 percent (Germany). Depreciation and divestiture operations did not begin until after the agreement on the forced administration of Greece. A rapidly implemented "haircut" would have necessitated a new round of massive rescue operations on the part of European institutions and the various national governments, in order to avert the collapse of financial capital in the core states of the EU.

If no one else, the European actors must at least have realized, as early as May 2010, that the objectives outlined in the troika agreement could not possibly be achieved. From their perspective as stakeholders, what was decisive was simply that Greece's national bankruptcy had been delayed. But Greece was also to serve as a chilling example by which to convince the governments of the EU's other over-indebted peripheral countries that they needed to impose rigorous austerity programs of their own, if they wanted to avoid the establishment of a *de facto* forced administration on the lines of the troika. By contrast, the Greek government seems, at least initially, to have genuinely believed in the possibility of achieving the objectives outlined in the agreement. After all, these objectives corresponded to their own economic and financial policy models. The Greek government's bellicose and patriotic justification of its severe austerity measures was no sham. Nevertheless, the government invoked the chaotic scenario of the drachma being reintroduced and triggering hyperinflation; it did so with an eye to disciplining the leaders of the formerly socialist party. Differently from what many former activists of the party left had predicted, PASOK encountered no difficulties until it passed the fourth of its restructuring programs in February of 2012. The main reason for this seems to have been that hopes of a generous debt cut were not fulfilled.

The objectives outlined in the troika agreement were illusionary. In implementing its policy of deflation, Greece merely aggravated its recession. There developed a social situation that was increasingly reminiscent of the Great Depression of the 1930s. As the social security system was gutted, traditional family-based networks of mutual support gained in importance. Eighty percent of all young people moved in with their parents again. Young university graduates and computer scientists found refuge in their fathers' small businesses: retail stores, fishing businesses, taverns, taxi companies, etc.

In May of 2011, the leaders of the troika commission returned to Athens to join their local staff in monitoring the progress of their aid and austerity programs. They were granted unrestricted access to the offices and databases of all Greek ministries and public authorities. On 8 June 2011, they summarized the results of their inspection in an evaluative report.[9] In the report, they admitted that the ongoing and worsening recession had rendered earlier objectives illusionary. But they also blamed the halting implementation of the austerity program for Greece's failure to achieve the targeted levels of economic consolidation. Nevertheless, they declared themselves willing to implement a medium-term finance program under which the consolidation period would be extended until 2014, by which time Greece was expected to finally conform to the criteria stipulated in the Maastricht Treaty. Moreover, the repayment terms would be rendered less severe. The interest charged for the troika's loans was lowered to 3.5 percent, and the repayment periods were extended to between 15 and 30 years, including a grace period of up to ten years. These measures amounted to a first, albeit veiled form of debt relief. The level of debt relief corresponded to 21 percent of the par value of Greek government bonds. Moreover, Greece's creditor banks were to be involved in the debt relief measures.

Yet the Greek negotiators were made to pay a high price for these minimal concessions.[10] They were forced to implement a second set of austerity measures, characterized not just by further cuts to wages and social spending, but also by direct intervention in the public sector. This involved, first and foremost, a comprehensive hiring freeze: for every ten employees entering retirement, only one was to be replaced. In addition to this, as many as 50,000 public sector employees were to be transferred to rescue companies, where they would continue to receive 60 percent of their previous salary for a one-year period, after which they would join the ranks of the unemployed. The troika commission also made it clear that this was to be no more than a first step towards a comprehensive restructuring of Greek labor market and welfare policies. During the months to come, "project managers" from an EU "task force" would draft standard employment contracts for the public sector, privatize healthcare, deregulate the pension system and lower minimum wages.[11] Thus there emerged the outlines of a comprehensive restructuring program for Greece's labor and welfare policies. Greek society was to be subjected to a radical "shock therapy." It was to be made to conform, within the briefest of time spans, to standards it had taken the deregulating authorities of the EU's core states more than two decades to impose.

Yet in the troika commission's view, Greece could look forward to a genuine "new beginning" only if it went beyond these measures by ridding itself of its substantial public assets, ideally at a similar pace. This was why the troika managers forced the PASOK government to set up an authority that would act as national trustee and oversee the comprehensive privatization of public infrastructure, state-owned real estate and state-owned telecommunications and public utility companies. The list of privatizations reads like a catalog of horrors. It included choice items such as Athens International Airport, the port of Piraeus and the OTE telecommunications company, but also water providers, the Greek Post Office Bank, the state-owned armaments company and areas on Rhodos and other islands that were to be developed for tourism.[12] By contrast, the traditionally conservative cornerstones of Greek statism, the state church and the military, were spared. The orthodox state church's extensive real estate assets were not to be touched. Similarly, the military was made to suffer only a minimal reduction of its arms expenditure. This reduction is to begin in 2013 and will amount to 0.1 percent of GDP. By comparison, medical drug expenditures are to be cut by 0.4 percent.[13]

It was only when the privatization plan was accepted by PASOK's Evangelos Venizelos, who had exchanged his position as Minister of Defense for that of Minister of Finance, that the leaders of the troika commission declared themselves willing to recommend disbursal of the fifth loan instalment and initiation of a second loan program. Under a medium-term finance plan covering the period until 2014, the privatizations are to yield 50 billion euros; cost-cutting measures and tax hikes are to yield an additional 28 billion euros. In return for acceptance of the privatization program, the creditors were advised to increase the volume of the existing loan program by 109 billion euros; it was also recommended that the creditor banks participate in the debt cut by renouncing claims of up to 50 billion euros. Ratification of this second agreement by the Greek negotiators once more took the form of a race through parliament. By contrast, the creditors represented by the troika did not ratify the agreement until several weeks later; it was not until 21 July that the agreement had cleared its last hurdle. Meanwhile, the next debt cut was already being prepared. But since it too was expected to produce major collateral damage, putting European creditor banks and the eurozone's other over-indebted peripheral countries at risk, an agreement was reached to set up a European Financial Stability Facility (EFSF) that would operate independently from the European Central Bank. What lies behind this ponderous name is nothing but a stabilization fund for the EU, charged with henceforth taking action even before economic developments come to a head. The EFSF is to provide emergency credits, buy up risk-fraught government bonds, perform open market operations and recapitalize ailing banks. It was only after the EFSF had been set up and provided with a total of 440 billion euros[14] that an "orderly" process of debt restructuring (with Greek debt being cut by about half) was considered feasible.

Consistent implementation of the second austerity plan amounted to an open attack on public sector employees, probably PASOK's most important electoral base. For this reason, Papandreou and Venizelos now began to play for time. When the troika commissioners returned to Athens in August of 2011, Greece's top politicians explained to them that the recession had continued to worsen and might get entirely out of hand if the austerity programs were implemented too rapidly. They asked for the budget consolidation objectives to be watered down further; they also requested early payment of parts of the second loan package.

Heated arguments ensued, but the leaders of the delegation sent by the European Commission, the European Central Bank and the IMF refused to budge. They insisted on prompt readjustment of public sector wages, the initiation of mass layoffs (i.e. the transferal of public sector employees to rescue companies) and the handing over of state-owned companies to the privatization authority, now headed by the director of Euro-Bank's investment department (Euro-Bank is part of the Latsis group). The German government made it clear that in the case of further procrastrination, it would declare itself in favor of Greece's accelerated bankruptcy and exit from the eurozone. This threat caused Athens to panic. Papandreou and Venizelos came to the conclusion that the troika had the upper hand. In the second half of September, the first public sector employees were transferred to a rescue company and the "National Welfare Fund" organized the first privatization auctions. In order to compensate for the loss of tax revenue the recession was causing, a number of special taxes were introduced, placing further strain on private households that were already suffering from the effects of the crisis. The most important of these new taxes were a special tax on all real estate (including residential estates), a surcharge for freelance professionals and a solidarity surcharge that reminded many historically conscious Greeks of the head tax (*charatsi*) introduced under Ottoman rule.

In mid-October, the troika presented its evaluation report for the third quarter of 2011. The troika issued a communiqué stating that the stabilization program had by and large been implemented, so that disbursal of the sixth loan instalment (8 billion euros) might be contemplated. Once again, the troika was playing for time. It was waiting until the stabilization fund was in working order. Then, it would be possible to avoid the collateral damage a major debt restructuring operation was expected to produce. That Greek financial corporations would not be able to survive such an event without the aid of the EFSF and the European Central Bank was evident, for they would have to depreciate their 48.2 billion euros worth of Greek bonds by at least 60 percent, i.e. by almost 29 billion dollars. By contrast, French and German financial corporations were now well prepared, having divested themselves of the bulk of their bonds by selling them to the European Central Bank and their national banking sectors. By late 2011, France risked losing no more than 9.4 billion euros. Moreover, only four of the country's major banks would be seriously affected, and these were banks such as the Franco-Belgian Dexia Bank, who were already in a precarious situation anyhow, for other (structural) reasons. In Germany, twelve banks were still holding Greek bonds worth 7.6 billion euros, but they had already partly adjusted the value of these bonds. Such prompt risk containment had only been possible because Germany's state-owned Reconstruction Loan Corporation and the nationalized bad bank Hypo Real Estate had purchased 22 billion euros worth of Greek bonds from Germany's private banks.

The Papadimos Interim Government and the Radicalization of the Troika's Austerity Course

The troika supervisors called for a further stepping up of austerity and prompt implementation of the envisioned deregulation measures. They justified their rigid stance by pointing out that the Greek economy would continue to experience negative growth in 2012, rendering obsolete the budget objectives that had been revised just a few months earlier. For the first time, there was talk of asking Greece's private creditors, who still held 60 percent or about 200 billion euros worth of Greek bonds in the fall of 2011, to waive a substantial part of their claims. Moreover, this debt cut was to be agreed upon on a "voluntary basis", and it was to comprise about 50 percent of the par value of the bonds. It was only if this additional condition was satisfied that national bankruptcy would be avoided, according to the supervisors. And national bankruptcy needed to be avoided, they added, since it would entail redemption of the globally distributed risk premiums (credit default swaps) associated with Greek bonds, thereby wreaking new havoc on the international financial markets.

On 26 October 2011, the eurozone's heads of state and heads of government backed the troika's revised program of action and reached a third agreement on loans and austerity measures with the Greek government. Papandreou and Venizelos committed themselves to a further intensification of the process of "internal depreciation." They also promised prompt implementation of mass public sector layoffs, vigorous tax collection and the elimination of the obstacles to privatization that had in the meantime become apparent.[15] In parallel with this newly restrictive policy, negotiations with private creditors were to be taken up, with an eye to making the creditors agree to "voluntarily" relinquish 50 percent of the par value of their bonds by the end of the year. This however would only be possible if the troika made available a new set of loans providing a total of 130 billion euros.[16] This money was required both to finance the process of debt restructuring and to compensate for budget deficits that were expected to increase further, at least for the time being. It was hoped that in the medium term, this would allow Greece to reduce its public debt, now at 160 percent of GDP (more than 350 billion euros), to 120 percent by 2020, without impinging upon the Greek economy's capacity to service its existing debt to global investors and the interest accruing thereon. In addition to this, measures were taken, on the level of the eurozone, to reduce the agreement's vulnerability to the speculative interventions of global investors. These measures included the expansion of the EFSF's range of application, the recapitalization, by the European Central Bank, of 70 strategically important eurozone banks and an agreement rendering the imposition and monitoring of budgetary discipline more efficient within member states.

In the days following the passage of the third consolidation and loan package, parts of Greece's political class began to realize that the loan and debt restructuring conditions stipulated therein would further aggravate the economic crisis, in addition to subordinating the country to the diktat of its creditors for more than a decade. This was a grave prospect. Moreover, on 28 October, an important date in the history of Greece's national resistance,[17] spectacular mass protests occurred. In the course of these protests, the PASOK government was accused of "national treason" for having bowed to the troika's demands. Prime Minister Jorgos Papandreou decided to organize a referendum on the agreement. It was quite probable that the referendum would lead to rejection of the agreement. Accordingly, the European architects of the Greek experiment and their media collaborators panicked. On 2 November, German chancellor Angela Merkel and French president Nicolas Sarkozy massively pressured Papandreou. They halted the promised disbursal of the sixth loan instalment until the referendum had been held – not without adding that the entire loan package would become obsolete if the plebiscite were to yield a negative result. It was easy for them to engage in this sort of blackmail, because they knew that by his decision to organize a referendum, Papandreou had isolated himself within the PASOK leadership. On 3 November, the Greek prime minister revoked his decision and called for the establishment of a "national unity" government. Earlier, key members of the political opposition had spoken out in favor of accepting the third consolidation and loan agreement. In fact, a strong majority of Greek parliamentarians voted in favor of it the next day, ensuring disbursal of the sixth instalment (8 billion euros) stipulated in the first credit agreement.[18] Immediately thereafter, Papandreou began negotiations with the leaders of the conservative opposition, in preparation for forming a new government. On the one hand, he was concerned with saving face when stepping down, something he would now inevitably have to do; on the other hand, he wanted to ensure that the conservative parties (Nea Dimokratia – ND – and the far-right Laos Party) shared responsibility for what was increasingly presenting itself as an attack on the vital interests of the overwhelming majority of the population.

On 7 November, Papandreou and ND's chairman Antonis Samarás agreed to install the former director of the Greek central bank and former vice president of the European Central Bank, Lukas Papadimos, as the new head of government. The new government also included Evangelos Venizelos, who had headed the Ministry of Finance until then. Along with the "technocrat" Papadimos, he represented the closest confidants of the troika and the most outspoken supporters of its austerity policies. Since the politically unaffiliated Papadimos enjoyed little popularity within Greece, due to his dubious role in Greece's admission to the eurozone,[19] Venizelos increasingly became the strong man behind the scenes. The parliamentary left – the SYRIZA alliance and the Communist Party (KKE) – rejected the transition government and called for new elections. But Venizelos, who had been Minister of Defence under Papandreou between 2009 and 2011, and who enjoyed the support of the right-wing coalition partners, succeeded in extending the transition government's time in power as far as possible, in accordance with the wishes of the troika. New elections were not to be held until 6 May 2012.

Greece's foreign private creditors were not convinced of the new Papadimos-Venizelos tandem's prospects of success. They continued their exodus from the Greek bond markets and caused the return on ten-year bonds, whose market value was declining constantly, to rise to 35 percent. The Greek banks, which were now holding about 50 billion euros worth of government bonds, also slipped further and further into the red, as the rapid decline in mass income was causing a steep increase in credit defaults. Moreover, small investors were increasingly choosing to liquidate their savings; in September and October alone, they withdrew a total of 14 billion euros from their bank accounts. These were the last reserves the lower and middle classes disposed of. They were depending increasingly on family-based support networks, as the official unemployment rate rose above the 20-percent mark and industrial production declined by 11.3 percent in December of 2011 alone. To this was added the ongoing deterioration of foreign trade. While some of the more competitive segments of the Greek economy – in particular, the shipping companies and oil refineries – remained relatively stable, exports and imports continued to decline. Due to the progressively rising premiums on commercial letters of credit, German foreign traders were increasingly writing Greece off. The protagonists of German foreign trade had in any case been working to shift the focus of their activities away from the eurozone ever since the outbreak of the European debt crisis.

Their expansion strategies focused increasingly on the most important of the newly industrializing countries.

In mid-December of 2011, the troika supervisors realized that the third consolidation package was built on sand, just like the previous two. The Greek economic and financial crisis continued to worsen, and even the National Bank of Greece, long considered the most stable of Greece's financial institutions, was now deep in the red. In the course of November, the country's budget deficit rose by 5.1 percent, reaching a total of 20.52 billion euros and rendering the revised budget consolidation figures illusionary. Instead of facing the consequences and finally acknowledging that the consolidation and loan program was merely accelerating the economy's downward spiral, the troika supervisors became vicious. Until now, they had always acted in the shadow of their Greek contractual partners, in order to conceal as best they could the fact that they were increasingly turning these contractual partners into the collaborators of a short-sighted creditor diktat. They now abandoned this reticence. From late 2011 and early 2012 onward, Poul Thomsen, the Danish chief negotiator of the International Monetary Fund, deliberately sought the attention of the public. He accused the new government of failing to observe the agreed schedule for its "reforms." He also pointed a finger at the Greek economy's increasingly evident structural deficits, arguing that Greece's declining competitiveness was ultimately even more serious than its spiraling public debt, insofar as it prejudiced the investment climate. Unit labor costs were far too high, he claimed. There could be no other remedy than adjusting wages and pensions to labor productivity, which in Thomsen's view was far too low. The more frequently he repeated his public criticism in January of 2012, the more concrete his specific requests became, eventually resulting in a comprehensive catalog. The measures he called for included a drastic lowering of minimum wages, the abolition of holiday and Christmas allowances, including in the private sector, and the curtailment of pensions.

By February of 2012, Greece's total debt had reached a volume of about 380 billion euros, of which about 210 billion were owed to private creditors, and 170 billion to the troika creditors. The debt was expected to increase still further by the end of the year, reaching a projected volume of 400 billion euros.

Confronted with these figures, Papadimos and Venizelos ostentatiously backed the *de facto* forced administration's ever-expanding catalog of demands. But they were increasingly losing their credibility with the Greek population, given the narrowing divide between the putative horror scenarios of national bankruptcy and the dramatic consequences of the austerity policies already in effect. Support for Papadimos and Venizelos was also visibly dwindling among their conservative coalition partners and, to an extent, within PASOK. Public awareness of the nature of the projected measures was growing. As it became clear that these measures would also affect the conservative electoral base (professional groups such as taxi drivers and pharmacists, who had hitherto been shielded by corporatist regulations, but also specific groups of pensioners and the employees of public transporation companies), the Nea Dimokratia and Laos delegates increasingly opted for a strategy of obstruction. Likewise, opposition from within the ministerial bureaucracy became stauncher.

The decision-making centers of the European Commission and the eurozone perceived these developments as significant warning signals. During the last week of January, they indicated that they did not consider the transition government of the "technocrat" Lukas Papadimos, which they themselves had helped establish, the last word. From Germany, there came the call to establish a "savings commissioner." Acting as "European Union budget appointee for Greece," he was to be given the power to veto any decision that threatened the consolidation course demanded by the country's creditors. As it turned out, this suggestion did not meet with the requisite support within the European leadership, and the Germans retracted a proposal that was all too reminiscent of their own historical transgressions. But the substance of their proposals remained the same. On 6 February 2012, Merkel and Sarkozy called for the establishment of a blocked account, reserved for the purpose of Greek debt servicing; the Greek government was to have no access to this account. In effect, they were openly declaring their lack of confidence in the transition government, which was publicly branded as unreliable.

The Fourth Austerity Program of 12 February 2012

In parallel with this foray, Merkel and Sakrozy confronted the Papadimos government with an ultimatum: they requested that the government accept and implement the fourth austerity program outlined, during the previous weeks, in the public statements of IMF negotiator Thomsen. This catalog of measures far outdid its predecessors in terms of its radical and uncompromising character. It was blatantly a product of the insight that the second and third austerity pacts would not be sufficient to bring about, at the requisite pace, a "cold" deregulation, flexibilization and precarization of Greek employment relations. The process of adjusting Greece's labour and wage policies to the standards of the EU's core countries was stalled. What was now envisioned in its place was a body of laws passed with the blessing of parliament. It was to give first priority to an immediate and comprehensive curbing of labor costs while simultaneously cutting down on social spending.

So far, the remnants of social security within the Greek public sector had been progressively eliminated, but now this was no longer enough. The full spectrum of the subaltern classes was now to be forced into the crucible of a post-Fordist low-wage policy. The first item on this agenda was the minimum wage received by about 500,000 Greek workers (10 percent of the working population). The minimum wage for adults was to be lowered by 22 percent (from 751 to 586 euros), the minimum wage for workers under the age of 24 by 32 percent. An important cumulative side effect of this measure would consist in a drastic reduction of unemployment benefits – to which Greece's unemployed workers are in any case only entitled for the duration of a year – as well as of other welfare benefits associated with the minimum wage. The abolition, within the private sector, of holiday and Christmas allowances, i.e. of the thirteenth and fourteenth monthly wage payments, was the second major item on the agenda. The third major savings measure consisted of slashing the last of the stable pension funds: retired employees of banks, electricity providers and telecommunications companies were to submit to their monthly payments being reduced by an average of 15 percent. A fourth item envisioned "opening up" the professions of taxi drivers, pharmacists and craftsmen. The protected status of these workers had allowed them to join the ranks of the middle class. They were now to be expropriated by means of the invalidation of their costly licences, thereby exposing them to the ruinous competition of putatively self-employed workers. A fifth item concerned public sector employees. Here, cuts had already been planned for some time, but the employees had largely been able to avoid the layoffs called for in the previous austerity programs. Now, they were no longer to be spared. Before the end of 2012, 15,000 of them were to be layed off; the "decruitment" of another 100,000 was planned for the following year. To these radical cuts were added further measures intended to lower medical drug and healthcare spending – the subsidies received by hospitals and health centers had already been slashed by 40 percent – eliminate grants to municipal and communal governments and continue the skeletization of the educational system. The privatization process, which had not been implemented as speedily as anticipated, was also to be tackled with greater vigor. These measures were expected to result in 4.4 billion euros worth of savings in 2012 alone.

In early February, and on the basis of these basic data, Papadimos and Venizelos reached an agreement over the new austerity program with the troika's leading representatives. On the weekend of 4 and 5 February, they then tried to win the consent of the coalition party leaders. In doing so, they assumed different roles. Papadimos outlined the putative disaster of an "unregulated" national bankruptcy. He did not limit himself to projecting the economic consequences of such an event, but also invoked the specter of unbridled social unrest. Venizelos's argument was that time was running out. He claimed that if parliament did not adopt the entire set of cost-cutting measures by next Sunday (12 February), the entire "rescue package" would be at risk. This, Venizelos said, was the outcome of a telephone conference with the eurozone's ministers of finance.

But the conservative camp's party leaders were only partly convinced by these arguments. There ensued several days of intense debate. Jorgos Karatzeferis, the chairman of the Laos Party, criticized the entire set of measures as a "humiliation for Greece" and refused to accept the pension cuts. ND's chairman Samarás pointed out that the cost-cutting measures would stifle the Greek economy altogether. The medicine, he said, was worse than the disease. Nevertheless, he backed down in the end, claiming later that he had tried to avert the worst of the projected hardships. The Laos Party eventually made up its mind to reject the measures, but Nea Dimokratia and PASOK decided on 9 February that they would support them, in spite of the purely cosmetic nature of the changes they had been able to impose. Supplementary pensions would not be abolished (the 325 million euros their abolition had been expected to save were to be saved by other budget cuts), and the thirteenth and fourteenth monthly wage payments would be retained. This, however, had no serious impact on the intended reduction of labour costs, as major wage subsidies were abolished instead,[20] and there was to be a general wage freeze until the unemployment rate had dropped to 10 percent. The lowering of the minimum wage was accepted, as was the concomitant reduction of unemployment benefits from 461 euros to an average of 322 euros a month. The combined effect was that of reducing the Greek wage fund by about 30 percent. Public sector employees were also affected by this kill-or-cure remedy. Not only was the envisioned quota of mass layoffs confirmed (15,000 immediate layoffs, and a total of 150,000 by 2015), but employees in state-owned companies lost their status as civil servants. Thus, contrary to Samarás' claims, no substantial changes had been made. The goal of combining additional budget cuts with a comprehensive and far-reaching reduction in wage income was fully achieved. This was projected to lead to a 3.1 billion euro reduction of public spending in the 2012 financial year, with a projected 14 billion euros saved by 2015. In addition to this, the treasury was to receive an additional 19 billion euros by 2015, thanks to a simplified system of taxation and the implementation of the privatization program, which had also been accepted in full, and which now included such choice items as the state-owned oil refineries.

Thus on the evening of 9 February, Papadimos was able to declare "mission accomplished" to the leading representatives of the European Central Bank, the eurozone and the International Monetary Fund. They however were not willing to content themselves with the assurance that nothing stood in the way of the austerity measures being passed by parliament on Sunday. Instead, they continued their game of cat-and-mouse, although this time, it was the head of the Eurogroup, Jean-Claude Juncker, who stepped to the fore. Recalling that new elections had been scheduled for April or May, he demanded that the chairmen of PASOK and ND provide him with a written assurance to the effect that they would continue to implement the austerity pact after the elections. They were also to classify as a liability the 325 million euros that needed still to be saved. Only if these conditions were met would there be any chance of the eurozone's ministers of finance agreeing to disburse the second loan (130 billion euros) at their meeting on 15 February. Olli Rehn, the European Commissioner for Economic and Monetary Affairs and the Euro, upped the ante by remarking that the option of a blocked budgetary account, which the Greek government would have no access to, was not yet off the table.

On 12 February, the Greek parliament debated the new austerity package. The parliamentary session was accompanied by intense mass protests and characterized by embittered verbal sparring matches. At times, the debate got thoroughly out of hand. Only 278 of the 300 delegates had shown up; most of those absent were members of the Laos Party. Twenty-two PASOK delegates and 21 ND parliamentarians joined KKE and SYRIZA in voting against the austerity diktat. They were promptly excluded from their parliamentary factions.[21] Given a vote of 199 to 101 in favor of the austerity package, its passage was never at risk. Nevertheless, the vote showed that the process of political polarization had reached the two major parties. Nor did ND chairman Antonis Samarás succeed in credibly justifying his change of course. His recommendation of saving Greece from disaster by voting in favor of the austerity package while simultaneously hoping for better times, during which the package might be renegotiated and corrected, was not convincing. As for the political representatives of Greece's creditors, they decided only a few days later that both Samarás and PASOK chairman Jorgos Papandreou should issue a written assurance that they would implement the austerity pact not just before, but also after the elections. The Eurogroup received these declarations of commitment on 15 February, along with a corrected savings plan in which the savings objective was increased by another 325 million euros. Polls showed that popular support for PASOK had dwindled to between 6 and 8 percent, but Nea Dimokratia had likewise been sucked into the maelstrom of political self-destruction; hopes that the re-elections might work out in ND's favor, due to the oppositional stance the party had taken until now, appeared increasingly unfounded.

The Negotiations with Private Creditors

As we have seen, the debate on whether or not Greece's private creditors ought to partially waive their claims had accompanied the loan negotations since the passage of the second austerity package in July of 2011. Until the fall, the private creditors had played no more than a marginal role, since the volume of bonds earmarked for deferral and reduced interest was initially quite modest. But this changed in the course of the negotiations on the third loan and consolidation agreement. Now, and for the first time, the troika's protagonists called on private bond creditors to relinquish half the par value of the 206 billion euros worth of Greek bonds held by them. The creditors were asked to negotiate this option with the Greek government. An official loan default ("credit event") and the concomitant mobilization of insurance premiums (credit default swaps) would have posed serious risks for the international financial markets, and particularly for those of the eurozone. To avoid these risks, it was proposed that the bonds currently held by creditors be swapped for new bonds with lower interest rates. This decision concerned all those financial investors who had not yet, or only partly, succeeded in divesting themselves of their increasingly worthless Greek bonds or transferring them to the public financial sector.

At the beginning of the new round of negotiations in October 2011, the concerned bonds, whose total par value was 206 billion euros, were held by a broad spectrum of investors. Institutional investors and hedge funds constituted the largest group, holding 98 billion euros worth of bonds. Next came the Greek banks (45 billion), European foreign banks (29 billion), the Greek pension fund (25 billion) and a group of non-European foreign banks (7 billion); a small group of individual investors brought up the caboose (2 billion).[22] After protacted debates, this highly heterogeneous group agreed to ask the internationally active Institute of International Finance (IIF) and its director Charles Dallara to conduct the negotiations.[23] Dallara received ongoing advice from IIF director and Deutsche Bank CEO Josef Ackermann; he was also advised by a settling committee consisting of experts from the transatlantic region's leading investment banks. Little of what occurred during the negotiations was made public. The business press and the relevant economic and financial news agencies provided only fragmentary information. Since we cannot wait for the documents produced during the negotiations to be made public, we need to attempt an interpretation of the more reliable pieces of information. In doing so, we may assume that the basic framework of the debt restructuring agreement had already been elaborated in the fall of 2011. It envisioned the old bonds (206 billion euros par value) being swapped against new bonds worth 70 billion euros. Moreover, the deal was to be made more appealing to creditors by providing them with 30 billion euros in cash or short-term bonds issued by the European stabilization fund, the EFSF. This last proposal shows particularly clearly that the private creditors were handled with kid gloves. Once the basic framework had been agreed upon, the details were fought out: the duration of the new loans and the interest on them. In order to reconcile the divergent interests of those he was representing, Dallara negotiated this point relentlessly. After some hesitation, he was willing to accept loan periods of up to 30 years. In return for this concession, he asked for at least 5 percent annual interest. The representatives of the Greek government were unable to accept this; they were not willing to concede more than 4 percent annual interest. The negotiations were discontinued several times; by late 2012, they had repeatedly threatened to fail altogether. But because the Greek economic situation continued to deteriorate, rendering obsolete the IMF data the austerity program, the troika loan and the envisioned debt restructuring measures were based on, the eurozone's heads of government eventually intervened. In late

January, they asked Dallara and the settling committee to show greater willingness to compromise. In the first week of February, a maximum annual interest rate of 4 percent was agreed upon. Then, in the context of the passage of the fourth austerity program, the Greek government upped the ante, requesting an interest margin of 3.5 percent and the replacement of the 30 billion euro cash payment by a short-term EFSF bond. This meant that when the new bonds (worth 70 billion euros) were issued, the private creditors would have to renounce 65 to 70 percent of the par value of the earlier bonds.

This was about as much as the Greek government could hope to achieve under a debt restructuring agreement that had been defined as voluntary. The government was now struggling to balance the claims of the eurozone and the expectations of private creditors with the Greek economy's own vital interests. More than ever, the eurozone's ministers of finance were insisting on an agreement that sidestepped the automatism of formal bankruptcy proceedings, as these would have dealt a serious blow to the unified currency. Under these circumstances, it was not possible to ask the heterogeneous group of private creditors to renounce more of their claims. If the negotiations failed and a credit event resulted, one group of private creditors, represented mainly by hedge funds, would have fared much better than the others, due to the ensuing disbursal of default premiums. Given this dilemma – which Greece of course shared responsibility for – the crisis-wracked Greek economy's need for a more extensive debt cut fell by the wayside. It was only in the days following the passage of the fourth austerity package that some exponents of Europe's leading economic bodies drew attention to this fatal development. For the first time, they asked that public creditors – whose claims totaled 180 billion euros – be made to participate in the debt cut. They recommended that the Greek bonds the European Central Bank had purchased at prices far below par value either be held until the due date, with the revenue then being channeled to the Greek treasury, or that they be passed on to the EFSF at their acquisition prices, in which case the revenue could also be used to relieve the Greek budget. Given the dramatically skewed combination of austerity pact, troika loan and debt restructuring negotiations, the idea of at least renouncing the profits anticipated from Greek bonds was perceived as out of the question. In any case, the sums this would have freed up would hardly have been sufficient for closing the loan gap, which the Greek economy's downward spiral was continuing to widen. Only a few days after the Greek parliament had passed the fourth austerity program, new projections were circulated, according to which the second loan package (130 billion euros) would have to be supplemented by at least another 15 billion euros, if the agreed goal of lowering the Greek budget deficit to 120 percent of GDP by 2020 was to be achieved.

By Order of the Financial Corporations: The Implementation of the Troika-Diktat until March of 2012

In the period from 15 to 20 February 2012, the troika program's three components were definitively codified. In the process, the Greek government had to consent to another far-reaching humiliation. On 15 February, following a telephone conference between the Eurogroup's ministers of finance, Greece was forced to agree to the creation of a blocked account. Apart from the instalments of the second troika loan, totaling 130 billion euros, significant portions of the state's running income were to be deposited there and used, first and foremost, to service the Greek debt. The Greek economy thereby relinquished the core component of its fiscal sovereignty, bowing definitively to the diktat of its public and private creditors. It was an open secret that both the Germans and Greece's private creditors considered the creation of such a blocked account a precondition for successfully concluding negotiations with the Greek government. The political leaders of the European Commission and the Eurogroup made no effort to disguise the fact that this move was primarily intended as a safeguard against the possibly unfavorable outcome of the new elections, scheduled for 6 May. Even a left-wing majority government would be unable to revise or even rescind the oppressive agreement.

Despite the Greek government's kowtow, the eurozone's ministers of finance issued no concrete decisions on 15 February. Significant political divisions developed within the eurozone. They resulted mainly from pronouncements by Germany's minister of finance, Wolfgang Schäuble, and prompted the Greek head of state, Karolos Papoulias, to respond harshly. Papoulias took the opportunity to point out that Germany, Finland and the Netherlands were giving in to pressure from their strong nationalist and conservative currents. These Eurogroup members were taking a particularly harsh and humiliating stance toward their Greek negotiation partners and seemed to consider even Greece's national bankruptcy a viable scenario. They were seconded by spectacular media reports, according to which the "failure of rescue measures for Greece" was becoming evident in the run-up to the next meeting of the Eurogroup's ministers of finance, scheduled for 20 February. The media pointed out that in their most recent report, the troika supervisors were questioning Greece's ability to continue servicing its debt and assuming that in spite of the private creditors' partial waiver of their claims, Greek public debt would still amount to 129 percent of GDP in 2020 (instead of the projected 120 percent).[24] As a result, a growing number of persons in the eurozone's key decision-making centers were pronouncing themselves in favor of delaying the decision until the EU summit scheduled for March, or even until after the new elections in Greece – notwithstanding the fact that the Greek government had to redeem bonds worth 14.5 billion euros during the second half of March, such that it would be forced to declare national bankruptcy if the second troika loan was not disbursed.

The boards of the German Central Bank and the European Central Bank seized the opportunity provided by this highly charged decision-making vacuum and began using procedural ploys to sidestep the debate on whether or not Greece's public creditors ought to be made to participate more strongly in a debt cut. The director of the German Central Bank, Jens Weidmann, the strong man behind Germany's monetarily disguised claims to European hegemony, condemned all calls for central bank participation in a debt cut as the cardinal sin of "monetary state funding."[25] Meanwhile, the European Central Bank proceeded to modify the registration numbers of its Greek bonds (50 billion euros par value) in such a way that they would be excluded from any debt restructuring package. The conditions on which the bonds were held were to remain unmodified, and only the possible profits were to be deposited on the blocked account. On 28 February, the European Central Bank went one step further: it announced that it would no longer accept Greek bonds as collateral, thereby eliminating this refinancing option for the Greek banks.[26] Thus the Greek government could no longer expect substantial help from the European Central Bank. On 20 February, a Monday, the eurozone's ministers of finance voted in favor of the loan to Greece. This was the second revision of the second, July 2011 "rescue package," which had followed the May 2010 aid program. The new loan consisted of 130 billion euros worth of financial aid, to be deposited on a blocked account of the Greek Ministry of Finance by the European stabilization fund (the EFSF) in quarterly instalments, until 2014. The money was to be used to compensate for the Greek budget deficit during the next three years, as well as to recapitalize the country's banks and pension funds. An additional 30 billion euros were provided to secure the debt restructuring agreement that Greece had simultaneously agreed upon with its private creditors. In return, the banks, investment funds and insurance companies represented by the Institute of International Finance relinquished 53.5 percent of the par value of their Greek bonds, amounting to about 107 billion euros. This was to be effected by exchanging the bonds against new, 30-year bonds with an average interest rate of 3.65 percent. In order to allow Greece to reduce its budget deficit to 120 percent of GDP by 2020, in spite of the fact that the economic situation had continued to worsen, the eurozone's ministers of finance lowered the interest on the first loan to an average of 2 percent and approved the European Central Bank's projected transfer of the profits earned on its Greek bonds to the Greek treasury. Greece's return services consisted in legal ratification of the blocked account, such that the Greek government would now have to service its debt and interest on a quarterly basis, and expeditious passage of the legislation required for implementation of the austerity agreement, prior to the EU summit in early March of 2012.

This was a diktat that benefited only the private and public creditors, at the expense of the Greek population. There was not the slightest intimation of supplementary measures to stimulate economic activity and ameliorate the rise of mass poverty. The loans that Greece was provided with, and which it was expected to repay with interest and compound interest, were intended solely for the servicing of the Greek debt and the country's banking and insurance sector. "The truth is that Schäuble & Co. have rescued the creditors, not the people," a *tageszeitung* editorialist wrote appositely.[27] Application of the diktat's thumbscrews had become a finely tuned process, as became clear in the days that followed. A series of implementation laws were speedily pushed through parliament by the Greek government, so as to allow it to close the remaining gap of 3.1 billion euros. These laws imposed the cuts to basic and supplementary pensions that had been halted on 12 February, and which were now expected to yield 625 million euros worth of budget savings. They also imposed a billion euros worth of further cuts to the medical drug and healthcare budget, curbed ongoing infrastructural investment by 400 million euros and restricted the expenses associated with a number of other budgetary items, on whose elimination the German minister of finance had insisted in return for release of the second loan package.[28] But things did not stop with the legislation by which these "prior action" objectives were pursued. The troika supervisors also kept a watchful eye on the Greek government's passage and dispatching of the concomitant implementation decrees and ministerial decisions. Everything worked smoothly. There were hardly any debates in parliament, and the parliamentary majorities were significantly larger than they had been on 12 February, when the overall package had been voted on. Moreover, the Greek ministerial and administrative bureaucracy had abandoned its earlier procrastination tactics. Nevertheless, it remained unclear just how much more leeway there was before Greece reached its breaking point. Thus when it came to implementing the core element of the "prior action" list, a further 22 percent reduction of the minimum wage, Prime Minister Papadimos chose to sidestep parliament and issue a cabinet decision.

Yet even these gestures of submission did not meet with unqualified approval within the decision-making bodies of the creditors. When the eurozone's ministers of finance met again on the occasion of the state summit in early March, they praised the Greek government's visible efforts, but refrained from straightforwardly announcing the release of the loan package. They limited themselves to approving selected parts of the package, which they considered essential to implementing the agreement between the Greek government and its private creditors, and which were expected to make a majority of investors settle for this agreement. For example, they disbursed the 30 billion euros worth of Eurzone funds that were supposed to make the agreement more attractive to investors. They also agreed to pay 5.5 billion euros worth of accrued interest and provide 23 billion euros to cover the losses Greek banks would suffer as a result of the debt cut. In addition to this, Mario Draghi, who had taken office as the new director of the European Central Bank on 1 November, did what he could to positively influence the private creditors, who had been given until 8 March to reach their decision. On 29 February, he provided Europe's strategically important banks with an additional 530 billion euros in the form of a three-year loan, the interest rate being fixed at 1 percent.[29] The purpose was not just to facilitate additional lending by other peripheral countries, but also to make the debt restructuring envisioned for Greek bonds more appealing to private creditors.

The measures had the intended effect. On 8 March 2012, the Greek debt restructuring offer was accepted by a sufficient majority of private creditors. A few days earlier, the International

Swaps and Derivates Association (ISDA) had stated that the debt cut was not likely to place a strain on credit default swaps.[30] About 86 percent of the private creditors holding bonds issued in accordance with Greek law gave their consent (the par value of these bonds was about 177 billion euros). Another 20 billion euros worth of bonds that had been issued in accordance with foreign law were swapped.[31] A few days later, the International Monetary Fund confirmed its participation in the second loan package and disbursed 28 billion euros. The Eurogroup's ministers of finance were slowest to respond: they did not disburse the rest of the loan package (71.5 billion euros) until 14 March. The Greek government needed this money for the loan redemption scheduled for 20 March, as well as for payment of interest and compensation of budget deficits. The money was not transferred to the new blocked account in Athens until the last minute.

Greek Society on the Brink

Greek society is now experiencing its fifth consecutive year of crisis. This is an extraordinary historical event, aggravated by the fact that since the spring of 2010, powerful supranational financial and economic institutions have been intervening in the Greek economy and accelerating its downward spiral. We have already touched upon some of the social consequences. The changes to Greece's labor-market and social policies are especially telling. Immediately prior to the outbreak of the crisis, in the spring of 2008, 7.7 percent of the Greek workforce was unemployed. At 22.4 percent, youth unemployment was almost three times as high (with persons between 15 and 24 years being classified as youth); moreover, there was the rise of the precarious "700-euro generation." In the course of 2009, adult unemployment reached the 10-percent mark, while youth unemployment rose to 32 percent. The third year of crisis brought unemployment rates of 16 and 35.6 percent for adults and youth, respectively. By the end of 2011, more than one million persons were officially unemployed (20.9 percent of the workforce), and one out of two youths was jobless.

Behind these increases, we discern a social catastrophe that unfolded before the eyes of the world. Like those of most of the eurozone's peripheral countries, the Greek social insurance system provides no form of protection against the medium-term effects of unemployment. Unemployment benefits used to take the form of a monthly sum of 480 euros, disbursed for the duration of a year. As a result of the lowering of the minimum wage, this sum has also been lowered. After one year, payment of the already minimal sum ceases altogether. Because unemployment benefits are so low, the process of downward social mobility sets in within just a few months. The unemployed become unable to pay their rent, mortgage and electricity and heating bills, and they are evicted from their apartments and houses. As a rule, they are able to move in for a time with their friends or relatives. But this is only a temporary solution, as the consequences of the government's austerity policy soon catch up with the people around them. The evicted end up on the street or in homeless shelters. As early as 2010, homelessness increased by 20 percent in the Athens-Piraeus region and other major cities. By the winter of 2011/2012, about 100,000 persons lacked proper shelter – 35,000 in Athens alone. The number of persons living in absolute poverty – persons who can no longer afford a heated apartment and a hot lunch – was at least tripled. Chronic malnutrition is spreading, mainly among the children and the elderly in working-class neighborhoods. In the winter of 2011/2012, the spread of hunger was curbed only thanks to the extensive activities of Orthodox Church congregations and some non-governmental organizations. The church congregations alone are currently providing more than 250,000 persons across the country with food on a daily basis. In the Athens region, there is also the aid organization Klimaka, which manages several homeless shelters and provides homeless persons, who typically camp out in groups, with blankets and food.

But this rapid process of immiseration was not caused by mass layoffs alone. Other factors also played a role, and they have become increasingly important since the implementation of the first, May 2010 austerity program. First and foremost, there are the progressive pension cuts, which in many cases have pushed monthly pension payments below the 500-euro mark, leading to a strong increase in old-age poverty. The minimum pension has even been lowered to 300 euros. Families with several children have also been hard hit. They must deal not only with rising unemployment, but also with massive wage cuts and a simultaneous increase in consumer and energy taxes and special taxes. As a result of these developments, the average income of working-class families had in many cases been slashed in half by late 2011 and early 2012. Thus more than a fifth of Greek society has slipped below the official poverty line. In concrete terms, this means than more 2.2 million people are no longer able to ensure the basic reproduction of their family life. The third group of the "new poor" (*neoftochi*) comes from the middle class. The Greek economy rests on about 930,000 small businesses and family businesses with four employees or less. Of these, 130,000 craft and service enterprises and 110,000 retail businesses have gone bankrupt over the past two years.

This has not just led to a steep increase in unemployment; it has also ruined some 240,000 self-employed families and small firms. Many of those affected have also had to default on their mortgages, thereby losing their homes. Consequently, the highly qualified young persons who found refuge in the family businesses of their parents after 2008/2009 have since been forced to search for new options. In the course of 2011, there developed a broad pattern of emigration. It was initially driven by the return of legal and illegal immigrants – Albanians, Rumanians and Poles – to their countries of origin. But in the meantime, thousands of highly qualified Greeks have decided to seek greener pastures in the core states of the European Union, as well as in Canada and Australia.

The social composition of the group of persons living in absolute poverty has changed dramatically over the past two years. At the outbreak of the crisis, this group consisted almost entirely of undocumented immigrants, drug addicts and the mentally ill. At first, their ranks were bolstered by the lower segments of the Greek working class: welfare-dependent pensioners, families with many children and unemployed persons. In the meantime, however, public sector employees have also been sucked into the maelstrom of downward social mobility. They have either been layed off in anticipation of privatization – as in the case of the formerly well-paid employees of the state-owned railway company OSE – or they have been forced into extremely low-wage employment. The decline of the middle classes occurred in parallel with this. Due to a chronic lack of capital, their craft, service and retail businesses were unable to survive the abrupt contraction of domestic demand and mass consumption. Today, it is not unusual for impoverished computer programmers to approach aid organizations and request shelter with their laptops under their arms.

During the first two years of the crisis, hundreds of thousands of Greeks participated in largely peaceful protests against the austerity policies the political class and the troika were imposing, policies that merely aggravated the crisis. A minority of young people – mainly undocumented immigrants and precarious workers from the extraparliamentary left – did not content themselves with non-violent demonstrations.[32] Despite providing some remarkable impulses, they did not get very far. They did not succeed in breaking up the ranks of the parliamentary and union-based left, which was hostile to them, and the security police discredited their agenda by means of systematic infiltration. As a result, there was no consolidation of social resistance on the level of the masses. In spite of a series of general strikes and recurrent mass protests – most recently, on the occasion of parliament voting on the austerity programs of November 2011 and February 2012 – resignation, apathy and helplessness increasingly gained the upper hand. Greek society has already experienced – and ultimately survived – a number of crises throughout its history. But this time, the outcome is particularly uncertain. Because no one can say what the future will bring, people's outlook becomes more and more somber and the hope that things will change for the better, at least in the medium term, is dwindling. In such a situation, recourse to Greek society's traditional structures of solidarity – networks of kin, the forms of mutual aid found in the proletarian strata of the population and the refuge provided by rural areas – becomes less viable. So far, these structures have staved off the worst, and emigration is presenting itself as a survival option to many people, as it has during earlier crises. But these options presuppose energy and intact social networks, two things that are beginning to be in short supply.

Instead, aggression and desperation are increasingly shaping everyday life. They are combining to produce a new kind of social pathology, which is further aggravated by the erosion of the healthcare system.[33] Most unemployed persons no longer have health insurance and are relying on medical aid organizations such as Doctors Without Borders, whose voluntary staff formerly dealt only with undocumented immigrants. Clinics and health centers now stock only half of 800 essential drugs; mortality among seriously ill and handicapped people requring costly medication is on the rise.

At the same time, violent crime and prostitution are spreading in many neighborhoods. Conditions in the country's overcrowded prisons are disastrous. Undocumented immigrants are increasingly being attacked by violent right-wing mobs. Domestic violence against women and children has risen dramatically. Greece's suicide rate – traditionally one of the lowest in Europe – has doubled: middle-class men who have been socially marginalized within just a few months are especially vulnerable. Whichever way we look: the majority of Greek society is living on the brink.

But what about the wealthy middle class? It has also suffered some losses, as emerges, for instance, from the figures recently published by the Latsis clan's financial holding company EFG International.[34] But the losses and write-offs suffered by Greece's capital asset owners have tended to be due to the global effects of the crisis, and they have remained limited. The shipping and financial dynasties that emerged during the postwar boom had already successfully internationalized themselves long before the outbreak of the crisis, shifting their centers of operation to Switzerland and the financial metropolises of the European

Union. To the extent that they still play any role within the Greek banking sector, their interests have been defended by the troika, which has earmarked vast amounts of its loan packages for the recapitalization of the Greek financial sector. The situation is different for the social stratum of the newly wealthy, which only took shape during the boom of the 1980s or following Greece's admission to the eurozone. This stratum had not yet developed any international networks when the crisis began. During the years prior to the crisis, they engaged in tax fraud that reduced the state's revenue by an annual 30 to 35 billion euros. The wage-dependent minority was taxed rigorously, being unable to engage in fraud due to the automatic collection of their payments. Following the outbreak of the crisis, the new upper classes proceeded to transfer a growing share of their capital assets abroad. According to conservative estimates, the volume of the assets transferred is somewhere between 80 and 90 billion euros. In spite of clamorous announcements by the troika supervisors and members of the political class, nothing was done to stop this exodus from the crisis until quite recently. But such an asymmetrical approach was not sustainable in the long run. The stratum of the newly wealthy will not be entirely unaffected by the measures recently taken to restructure Greece's fiscal authority; we may see some pawns being sacrificed soon. They may include Lavrentis Lavnertiadis, often presented as the social climber par excellence. During the last economic boom, he built an empire of chemical, pharmaceutical and media companies, as well as a private bank (Proton). The Greek judiciary is now accusing him of having resorted to criminal methods to transfer 700 million euros abroad.[35] Even if there should be a trial, it will remain an isolated case – absent a far-reaching political sea change.[36] The troika's decision-making centers and their abettors in Athens are not contemplating any substantial correction of the policy they have pursued thus far. The subaltern classes are expected to continue shouldering the burdens that result from the crisis.

Interim Conclusion: The Consequences of the Austerity Policies

Whoever has fairly regularly followed the trajectory of the Greek crisis in its national, European, and world economic contexts has come across both familiar and surprising facts. Among the latter was the closely synchronized crisis management of the Greek government, the European institutions and the International Monetary Fund. While the globally coordinated anti-crisis programs of past years were characterized by resolutely anti-cyclical monetary and fiscal policies and constituted an attempt to avoid the catastrophic mistakes of the 1930s,[37] in the case of Greece the opposite was evident from the very outset. What was going on? Did Greece, a relatively small economy in southeastern Europe, serve as a testing field for the return to budget restrictions, in spite of the fact that such methods had immensely aggravated the major crisis of the 20th century? Or was this a territorially limited punitive action of the European Union's ruling elites, who used the support of the IMF to implement an exemplary "shock therapy" and speed up the adjustment of the peripheral member states to the deregulation of labor and social policies evident in the core states of the European Union?[38]

Be that as it may, the Greek case quickly proved to be a cross-roads and a lesson – as well as a black box of unpredictable developments. Numerous laws have been violated during the implementation of internationally coordinated programs that have primarily targeted Greece's lower and middle classes, and it is rather debatable whether the ruling elites have been fully aware of the consequences of their actions. We are obviously dealing with a melange: the monetary and fiscal policy specialists' tunnel vision coincides with the multilateral policy-makers' ideological narrow-mindedness and the capital asset owners' boundless greed. The following interim conclusion tries to grasp the main scenarios that make up the Greek tragedy taking place before our eyes.

The Monster of Instrumental Reason

The first thing an attentive observer will notice is the narrow-mindedness of the specialists involved. Surveying the IMF memorandums on Greece and the troika commission's evaluation reports, one soon realizes that the authors' thinking is structured along two central axes: first, they give unconditional priority to budget consolidation; second, they want to ensure the return of the Greek economy to the free bond markets as soon as possible. All other economic parameters are subordinated to these reductive objectives. On this basis, the authors pursue macro-economic "structural adjustment" at all costs, in order to secure the returns on bonds signed by private and public creditors and rule out scenarios of debt restructuring resulting from a formal declaration of bankruptcy or negotiations. The experts of the IMF's Fiscal Affairs Department (FAD) retained this approach even when the triad region's debt crisis intensified dramatically in the fall of 2010. In September 2010, for instance, they opposed rising speculation about possible debt restructuring in Greece and explicitly ruled out any kind of debt cut.[39] For them it is beyond question that developed national economies facing over-indebtedness can be brought back on track by a mixture of budget consolidation, deregulation of labor market and social policies and privatization. They did not care whether their object of intervention was prospering or going through a crisis. Theirs was the static structural model used by IMF cadres since the 1980s. These IMF cadres made emergency credits conditional on implementation of their model, whether they were dealing with developing and newly industrialized countries in the south or with eastern European transition states.

With this credo in mind, the IMF staff led by Poul Thomsen set to work in the spring of 2010. From the outset, Thomsen was in charge of collecting the main macro-economic data and using them to define medium-term objectives. The task forces of the European Commission and the European Central Bank did the groundwork for him. The IMF team knew, of course, that Thomsen's focus on budget consolidation and the return of Greek bonds to the free bond markets depended on one decisive parameter: the overcoming of the recession. However, it was sure it could positively influence even that variable, since it believed overall structural adjustment of the economy, enforced through the instrument of budget consolidation, would rapidly restore Greece's competitiveness and increasingly allow the country to service its debt on the basis of export and current account surpluses. The result was a notorious calculated optimism with regard to the resumption of economic growth.[40] The team's first prognosis was based on the IMF experts' assumption that the Greek economy would be heading for a positive GDP development from late 2011 on. In later evaluation reports, the IMF experts projected that this reversal would occur one year later. Not until the fourth status report did they admit that the recovery process was lagging behind significantly, yet they continued to grossly underestimate the obstacles to renewed growth. In December 2011, they retained their calculated optimism and projected that after a year of zero growth in 2013, the Greek economy would grow again in 2014 (by 2.5 percent; see the table on page 92).

We should assume the leading officials at the Fiscal Affairs Department, the staff of the IMF's European Department and the members of the Athens task force are all well-educated economists who know their trade and can look back on years of experience in dealing with over-indebted national economies and imploded transition states.[41] Yet their skills do not save them from a behavioral syndrome the exponents of Critical Theory called "instrumental reason." The IMF experts are committed to a static structural model that consists of arbitrarily defined parameters and objectives, ignoring the overall economic dynamics of their object of intervention. The result is a coherent and efficient complex of quantifying relations, which may develop a potential for destruction, due to the arbitrary nature of the underlying precepts. The austerity programs' architects do not seem to mind that their methods aggravate the crisis. In the case of Greece, the ongoing quarterly decline of GDP forces them to periodically revise their fiscal parameters, but their conceptual framework remains unaltered. Their instrumental reason is calibrated in such a way that they are not able to apprehend what any other observer can see: the crisis-aggravating effects of their austerity policies. Thus fiscal revenue's downward spiral picked up more and more speed in the spring of 2011. The austerity policies stifled mass consumption and aggravated the recession. As tax revenue declined, the budget deficit grew even further, necessitating a new round of austerity measures.

Nevertheless, the destructive "structural adjustment" imposed on the Greek economy does have a "rational" core. The IMF experts do not consider their "shock therapy" an end in itself, and they do not apply it out of cynicism. Rather, there are power interests involved, and the international organizations' technocrats bear a double burden. On the one hand, they see themselves as global crisis managers; even prior to the outbreak of the current world economic crisis, they tried to distinguish themselves as "fire fighters" who get down to work and stabilize the world system. On the other hand, they have internalized the interests of global investors, to the extent that these investors are engaged on the market for state bonds, as they are in the case of Greece. Understandably enough, the creditors of over-indebted national economies that are slipping into bankruptcy want to be reimbursed if at all possible. This usually proves difficult, and so global institutions intervene to ensure, via their structural adjustment programs, that the interests of financial investors are protected, and that debt cuts dividing the losses between creditors and debtors are avoided. Banks and investment funds appreciate the IMF as an instrument of risk protection and loss minimization. New studies show that the IMF has increasingly substituted debt restructuring procedures with structural adjustment programs over the past thirty years.[42]

Since its formation in the 14th century, the capitalist world system has known national bankruptcy in all its forms. Throughout capitalist history, national bankruptcy has been an instrument of debt liquidation and for the overcoming of financial crises. It can be attributed more or less solely to the IMF that national bankruptcies have become less and less frequent in past decades – despite the rapid increase in financial crises. As a result, capital asset holders are made to pay less and less often. The costs of financial crisis are passed on more and more rigorously to the national economies' lower and middle classes. Periodical capital destruction is increasingly replaced by austerity programs that guarantee the "ongoing" plunder of the subaltern classes.

Deflation and Inflation: A Collective Exploitation Squeeze

But the IMF experts were not the only actors in Greece's tragedy. They enjoyed the support of European Central Bank (ECB) and European Commission task forces, both led by Germans. Klaus Maruch is the head of the ECB's Department of Economic Development in the EU Member States. He won his spurs while working closely with Otmar Issing, the former chief economist of the German Federal Bank, and later of the ECB. Matthias Mors entered the European Commission after completing his academic training in 1984. During his time in Greece, he worked under Olli Rehn, the European Commissioner for Economic and Monetary Affairs and the Euro, as director for the national economies of EU member states. Maruch and Mors were put on an equal footing with Thomsen, the head of the IMF delegation. The three teams collaborated closely and smoothly at their headquarters, the Athens Hilton. While Thomsen's task force focused on the objectives of the structural adjustment program, the staff of the ECB and the European Commission procured data and documents relevant to the ongoing fiscal and economic evaluation of the austerity program and its practical implementation from Greek government departments and agencies. They covered all key areas of the Greek economy: finances, tax policies, labor markets, welfare, state-run enterprises, but also the complex administrative hierarchy and the health service.

The two European task forces widened the conceptual framework of the multilateral intervention decisively. The European Commission and the ECB had temporarily adopted the globally controlled anti-crisis programs of the G20 group and the US Federal Reserve System, but in spring 2010 they returned to the principles of European "stabilization policies." Although the crisis had not been overcome, the old concepts that had dominated European fiscal and economic policy since the establishment of the ECB and the eurozone were reintroduced: monetary policy was rigorously oriented toward price stability, and the central bank was exempted from economic regulation, with its statute prohibiting the purchase of government bonds and the granting of credit to the public sector.[43] This approach ruled out every possibility of anti-cyclically expanding the money supply and lending to the public sector. But since the crisis soon resurfaced and intensified dramatically in the countries of the European periphery, time-consuming and ineffective detours had to be taken, such as the establishment of the European Financial Stability Facility (EFSF). Worse still, national economies that had slipped into depression had nowhere to turn to other than the free bond markets when trying to obtaining the means to expand public credit. As a result, the refinancing costs associated with public debt increased rapidly. This means that countries such as Greece are trapped in two ways. First, they are part of a monetary bloc that functions just like the former gold standard system in that monetary and credit restrictions exacerbate the crisis. Second, this European successor of the gold standard system lacks instruments by which to compensate for current account deficits and prevent the range of unit labor costs from widening. As a result, the structural differences between different eurozone economies increased during the crisis, with deindustrialization, disinvestment and decreasing labor productivity rendering the economies of Greece and other peripheral countries uncompetitive.

We can safely assume that the Europeans in the troika commission never properly understood this. Because of their one-sided academic training and their previous professional practice, they were unable to transcend the ideological justifications for restrictive stabilization policies. Instead of critically reflecting upon the absurdity of what is effectively a gold standard system on the scale of the European Union, they projected that system's logic onto their object of intervention and stifled the Greek economy by implementing an austerity policy even harsher than that of the Brüning era.[44]

We can nevertheless identify certain power interests behind this variant of instrumental reason as well. Like their intellectual mentors around financial economist Otmar Issing and his Center for Financial Studies, the European troika emissaries are convinced the financial cornerstones of their deflationist, restrictive and low-wage programs are decisive for Europe's rise to the status of the world system's most competitive economic bloc in the world-system. They have unwaveringly retained this conviction until today, although the entire eurozone is now slipping back into recession, accelerating the decline of Greece and other peripheral states. Instead of pausing, they started to use a crowbar. Their motives are obvious. Greece's national bankruptcy would lead to the depreciation of the euro vis-à-vis other world currencies and destabilize the European banking system, putting a damper on utopian dreams of world hegemony. This is why the teams around Masuch and Mors have tried to delay Greece's insolvency as long as possible. They have struggled to win time and resorted to "irregular" measures such as increasing the capital stock of the European stabilization fund and creating a temporary glut of money by which to support European banks and protect the other threatened peripheral states from the "risk of infection." At the same time, private creditors were offered the opportunity to divest themselves of at least some of their government bonds. Should a debt cut still turn out to be necessary, creditors' losses would be curbed so as to preserve the prospects for stable and long-term European capital allocation.

These specific interests notwithstanding, there was still enough common ground with the agents of the International Monetary Fund. The austerity program was to be launched jointly, and could in fact be accelerated and radicalized insofar as it was packaged as an IMF-typical structural adjustment program. Furthermore, the teams of troika supervisors agreed that national bankruptcy needed to be delayed, and that the creditors' interests would have to be asserted as strongly as possible if it proved unavoidable.

These were the premises guiding the teams of troika supervisors and the multilateral institutions behind them as they set to work. As we have learned from the empirical survey above, they have so far launched four comprehensive sets of measures, lowering wages and cutting social spending with an eye to curbing public expenditure and restoring the Greek economy's competitiveness through an "internal depreciation." Following the first cuts in May 2010,[45] their approach become frightfully systematic. The first massive cuts to social spending were laid down in the June 2011 evaluation report, which outlined the agenda for the period until 2015.[46] Wages and salaries in the public administration are to be lowered by a total of 2,175 billion euros, by cutting jobs, extending working hours, abolishing bonuses and unpaid holidays and getting rid of all self-employed and contracted staff while simultaneously introducing part-time labor and setting up a rescue company in preparation for mass layoffs. During the same period, welfare benefits are to be slashed by 4,176 billion euros. A wide range of additional interventions also featured on the agenda. These included the introduction of systematic standardization and monitoring systems, cuts to supplementary pension schemes, cancellation of occupational disability pensions, the freezing and gradual lowering of basic pensions, cuts to benefits associated with employee insurance funds, special deductions for pensions above 1,700 euros per month and a lowering of the minimum pensions disbursed by other social insurance funds. Further cutback measures were outlined for the healthcare sector (with projected total savings of 1,739 billion euros), and other expenditures amounting to 1,015 billion euros were also to be eliminated. This catalog formed the basis for another social attack on the entire spectrum of the lower classes, culminating in the reduction of minimum wages, unemployment benefits, wages and salaries throughout the private sector, and in a further set of pension cuts that was imposed in February and March of 2012. Its synopsis reads like a new version, refined and systematized through the introduction of individual monitoring methods, of the emergency decrees of the Brüning era (1930–1932). The troika commission also spared no effort to swiftly replicate for Greece the "agenda 2010" that has been enforced in Germany since 2003/2004, and which is geared to the creation of a low-wage sector that aggressively proliferates from the lower to the higher echelons of the working class. The results achieved became apparent in the corresponding statistical parameters (see the statistical summary at the end of this text). Private consumption's consistent slowdown, evident since 2009, accelerated as implementation of the austerity programs began, reaching a negative 11 percent in 2011. At the same time, the unemployment rate increased. It reached a yearly average of 17 percent in 2011 and has been increasing further since. Particularly striking was the decline in the relationship of wages to labor productivity, which began in 2010 and will reach a negative 7.8 percent by 2012, according to forecasts. Anyone who believes this might be a first step towards the extremely low unit labor costs in the EU's core states should consider the figures on the expenditure of human labor required to generate Greece's GDP (labor productivity). The ongoing processes of deindustrialization and capital flight have brought technical and organizational innovation to a standstill; both have been declining since 2009, with the most dramatic drop (4.2 percent) occurring in 2011. In the wake of the austerity programs, the Greek economy's competitiveness has deteriorated further, wage cuts and mass layoffs notwithstanding; the process has in fact been so dramatic that Greece may revert to the status of a developing country in the near future.

But this was only one of the cornerstones of the austerity programs. The measures taken to increase state revenue are equally significant. The troika experts struggled to stay ahead of the austerity spiral they had themselves created, and which was causing a continuous decline in tax revenue. Supported by their collaborators within the Greek political class, they imposed a broad range of tax hikes. Instead of focusing on the upper classes and their 30 billion euros worth of annual fiscal fraud, the lower and middle classes were made to bear the brunt of these tax hikes. The first austerity program already featured two consecutive increases in sales tax (the total increase was from 19 percent to 23 percent); in addition to this, major tax exemptions were abolished and the taxes on fuel and heating oil were drastically raised. These interventions were followed, one year later, by a second set of measures. The elaborate strategy underpinning this second package can only be understood after reading the June 2011 evaluation report.[47] An increase in tax revenue totaling just under 6.1 billion euros was projected for the period between 2011 and 2014, with most of the increase occurring in 2011 (at least 2.45 billion euros) and 2012 (2.779 billion euros). The additional tax revenue was to stem from further increases in sales tax (for instance, the sales tax on catering services was raised to 23 percent), higher property taxes, a 5,000 euro cap on annual tax allowances, an additional consumption tax on natural gas and a motor vehicle surcharge. To this was added a further package targeting social insurance contributors and projected to generate about 3.1 billion euros worth of additional revenue. A general increase in healthcare and pension contributions was implemented on the basis of a new, unified collection system and complemented both by a specific increase in the contributions to supplementary pension funds and by a "solidarity tax" for self-employed workers. Yet even these measures did not satisfy the troika commission. In order to mobilize even the last remaining income reserves, the commission substantially increased the regional government revenue from taxes, fees and surcharges levied for authorization and approval procedures. Thanks to these measures, an additional 600 million euros were expected to pour into the state coffers by 2015.

Already hit hard by its constant decline in income, the bulk of the population began to feel the full impact of these measures from the summer of 2010 onward. Gasoline prices rose to 1.80 euros per liter, and the price of heating oil nearly doubled, from 0.60 to 1.10 euros. Food prices also rose across the board, and the cumulative effect of the new taxes, surcharges and higher social insurance contributions dealt the final blow. Since the summer of 2010, the Greek population has been paying the highest consumer taxes in Europe; social insurance contributions are also among the highest in the eurozone.

The result has been that since 2011, the cost of living has been higher in Greece than in Germany, for example. A year earlier, inflation had already reached an all-time high. At 3.1 percent, it was still significantly above the European average in 2011. The troika supervisors expect a sharp decrease after 2012 (see the statistical summary at the end of this text), but it is highly doubtful that this expectation will be satisfied. We are thus confronted with a surprising discovery: the austerity policies imposed on Greece have led to a combination of deflation and inflation that strikes a severe blow to the lower and middle classes. This combination of deflation and inflation accounts for the astonishing pace of Greek society's incipient pauperization. The majority of the population is confronted with a 50-percent deterioration of its standard of living.

The agents of the troika commission and their abettors, the executive boards of the multilateral institutions and the representatives of Greece's political class, bear full responsibility for the logic underpinning this dynamic process of mass impoverishment. In a joint effort, they have initiated the collective exploitation of Greece's lower and middle classes. They have achieved this by eliminating attested rights, via the skeletizaton of wage and social funds, and by expanding the taxation system. The crisis is spiraling ever faster, but the revenue transferred from the lower and middle classes to the state coffers are passed on to the private and public creditors. The rates of collective exploitation achieved each year are immense (see the statistical summary). In 2011, at least 6.6 percent of GDP, or 14.4 percent of total state revenue, were just to pay for the interest on government bonds.

Thus in the case of Greece – but also, increasingly, in that of the European Union's other peripheral states – the predictions formulated by far-sighted observers at the outbreak of the world economic crisis are increasingly becoming a reality. The costs of the crisis have been shifted to national budgets, and it is not the investors responsible for the misallocation of capital and credit that are made to pay for them, but the subaltern classes. Classical processes of capital destruction are suspended as far as possible, and replaced by the secondary exploitation of those who have already been exploited within the capital relation.

A Largely Fictitious Debt Cut

Since the ratification of the debt cut agreed on by the Greek government and its private creditors, the situation has changed significantly. In the first half of 2011, the decline of the Greek economy had reached such a dramatic scale that the European Commission intervened and challenged the IMF's, the ECB's and the troika commission's fundamental opposition to the inclusion of private creditors in the process of crisis intervention. The European Commission considered it advisable to address the private sector and develop a scenario of "voluntary" debt restructuring. The aim was to delay Greece's national bankruptcy, which was now deemed possible, and to stave off its incalculable effects on the European banking sector and the other peripheral eurozone states.[48] The European banking lobby was quick to support this proposal and recruit the Institute of International Finance (IIF) as its representative in the upcoming negotiations with the Greek government. On July 21, 2011, the EU summit approved a first IIF proposal – along with a revised austerity and loan program. The proposal was that creditors waive 21 percent of the par value of bonds due by 2020. In return, they were offered a bundle of conversion options including substantial EU guarantees, leading to the factual reduction of the Greek state debt by 7 to 9 percent. Soon after, it emerged that this operation would leave the creditors with considerable profits on the par value of their old bonds, and so the plans were shelved. Critics of any kind of "haircut" felt vindicated; in particular, IMF representatives emphasized that they had retained their role as mere observers with good reason.

However, in October 2011 the tide turned when the IMF experts rang the alarm on the sustainability of Greek debt in their quarterly report.[49] They were forced to admit earlier targets had become obsolete due to the deepening crisis, the related deterioration of the budgetary situation and the failure of structural adjustment to produce rapid results. Continuing the austerity and restructuring programs would increase state debt to 186 percent of GDP by 2013; the debt could not be expected to decrease to less than 152 percent by 2020, and even in 2030, it would still be at 130 percent. Faced with this outlook, even the IMF experts dropped their earlier opposition to a debt cut. They argued in favor of a debt cut by which private creditors would relinquish 50 percent of the par value of their bonds, or half of 200 billion euros.

In the empirical section of this pamphlet, we have provided a detailed account of the second round of debt restructuring negotiations that began in October 2011. We can now concentrate on the question of how large the sums waived by the creditors actually were: to what extent did they really participate in the amortization of the burdens of the crisis?

Following ratification of the debt restructuring agreement, private investors swapped their old bonds, each of which had a par value of 1,000 euros, for new Greek bonds with a par value of 315 euros, as well as for bonds issued by the European Financial Stability Facility (EFSF); the par value of the latter was 150 euros. The private investors thus raked in an EU bonus amounting to 15 percent of the former par value; in addition, they received 5.5 billion euros in cash from the troika to cover for Greece's outstanding interest payments. Their acquiescence was therefore rewarded with 46.5 percent of the former par value; the relinquished claims amounted to 53.5 percent of the former par value. On top of this, there were substantial dividend payments. It would however be overhasty to consider the depreciation of the private creditors' bonds an actual loss or an actual case of capital destruction, as most investors had not purchased their bonds at par value but at much lower market prices (see the statistical summary). After 2009, the market prices of Greece's two- to ten-year bonds were much lower than their par value, while interest rose significantly. Thus, prior to the negotiations on a debt cut involving public and private investors, investing in Greek bonds was highly profitable. Exact numbers are not yet available, but we can assume that, on average, private creditors did not lose more than 16 percent of the bonds' former par value, considering that their agreement to the "voluntary" debt cut was sweetened by the "bonus" of the EFSF bonds, as well as by reimbursement of suspended interest payments.

The debt cut was therefore largely fictitious. It resulted in the destruction of about 32 billion euros worth of monetary assets; the remaining 75 billion euros (out of the total write-off of 107 billion euros) were simply unrealized profit expectations. The main burden of debt amortization rested and continues to rest on Greece's lower and middle classes. This conclusion reveals the core objective of the protracted debt restructuring negotiations: the aim was to determine just how far the ante can be upped if the broad majority of the Greek population is to remain subjected to a "sustainable" form of organized exploitation for the next ten to fifteen years. Even Britain's conservative *Economist* thought this approach was too risky. Its editors repeatedly emphasized that private investors were being handled with kid gloves and that the multilateral creditors who withdrew from the debt cut altogether were doing the troika a disservice.[50]

A Mockery of Democracy

We have already described how Greece's political class cooperated with the troika in bypassing the institutions and structures of parliamentary democracy. The hasty passage of the first austerity program already involved several constitutional regulations being swept aside; they stood in the way of the establishment of what is de facto a forced administration. The procedure developed – drafting a "memorandum" agreement with the troika, helping to obtain a parliamentary majority for the agreement and then steamrolling its implementation by passing dozens of by-laws within a few days – was resorted to ever more routinely in June 2011, October 2011 and February 2012. In November 2011, when a parliamentary majority seemed doubtful, PASOK's and ND's party leaders joined the troika's decision-making bodies in hectic negotiations on the establishment of an interim government. The interim government was to help ensure a majority vote in favor of still tougher austerity policies. Yet the ensuing "technocratic" coalition government under financial economist Papadimos could no longer claim any political legitimacy. Consequently, it was unable to guarantee the kind of concerted and disciplined behavior the parliamentary factions had displayed until then. During the vote on the February memorandum, the representatives of the extreme right left the coalition, and more than forty members of parliament refused to follow the course set by PASOK and ND. Given this situation, the troika's executive staff went one step further and began to prepare for the time after the interim government's demission. It demanded a written guarantee from the party leaders of PASOK and ND that the austerity programs would be fully implemented even after the parliamentary elections. In addition, future governments were deprived of their budget sovereignty and the creation of a blocked account was decided, so as to ensure that creditors' repayment and interest claims would be given priority. Thus the principle of popular sovereignty, respected at least periodically under the parliamentary system, was suspended in the interest of the crisis management agenda, and future governments were reduced to puppet regimes serving the creditor interests represented by the troika. This third phase of the erosion of parliamentary democracy can be described as a preemptive Bonapartism that depends increasingly on a multilateral form of forced administration. To what extent these Bonapartist tendencies would lead to the abolition of existing parliamentary structures and their substitution by a puppet regime depended on the results of the May 2012 parliamentary elections. The political class and the multilateral institutions supporting it will not enact a complete break with the political constitution developed after the end of Greece's military dictatorship (1974), unless the sovereign elects a government that refuses the austerity and credit package and sends the forced administration constituted by the European Commission, the ECB and the IMF packing.

The political tendency towards the establishment of a Bonapartist puppet regime that gained momentum after the spring of 2010 displayed specifically Greek characteristics.[51] Greek parliamentarism is characterized by strong authoritarian elements. After the end of the military dictatorship (1974), the parliamentary system was hijacked by rival family dynasties. They substituted the ruling class' traditional division into republicans and monarchists by a clientelistic two-party system, thereby adjusting to the rules of parliamentarism. A system of rotation developed: the rival dynasties took turns at exercising political power, so that each of the two parties was able to form a government every other election year. Parliamentary politics and its system of norms were gradually adjusted to this model. As a rule, one of the two clan and party leaders advanced to the position of prime minister and headed the governing party's parliamentary faction, while the rival who had lost the elections confronted him as the leader of the oppositional party and its parliamentary faction. The party leaders' conceptual precepts seldom meet with much opposition from the members of his parliamentary faction, because these members are not legitimated by the party base. It is the party's executive committee that puts them on the electoral list. If they nevertheless violate factional discipline, the leader of the parliamentary faction can immediately expel them from the party; he merely needs to inform the speaker of parliament of their exclusion.

Moreover, the incumbent prime minister can dissolve parliament at any time, and at his own discretion. New elections can also be scheduled at short notice, since candidates are not chosen through time-consuming primary elections and delegate meetings. It is only the party leaders and their supporting executive committees who draft the list of candidates. Finally, clear-cut election results are guaranteed: after the elections, the victor is given fifty additional seats in order to ensure a clear parliamentary majority. Thus even substantial changes in electoral behavior have to this date never precluded one of the two major parties from coming out on top.

This oligarchic setup was one of the main reasons why it was possible to implement "memorandums" and austerity packages by means of regular parliamentary laws, rather than through emergency decrees. In the meantime, the date of the new elections was repeatedly postponed. This all goes to show that the agents of the Bonapartist puppet regime use Greek parliamentarianism's authoritarian elements methodically.

We can see how far the de-democratization of Greek society has already progressed from the massive cutbacks to labor and social legislation.[52] Representative democracy has always been supported by a broad set of social and labor regulations that alleviate the asymmetry of class relations far enough to provide the subaltern classes with the time reserves and livelihood security necessary for participation in public life. Between May 2010 and February 2012, this foundation was systematically eliminated, as a result of the four austerity programs. A sledge-hammer approach was used to accomplish within less than two years what had taken the promoters of low-wage policies and social expropriation twenty years to achieve in the core states of the European Union. Hundreds of legal regulations were used to wipe out achievements within social and labor legislation that workers and unions had struggled for over decades. Collective agreements on wages, working conditions and social protection were abolished. The "National General Labor Agreement" was drastically whittled down, and even sectoral labor agreements are now up for renegotiation. Minimum standards for particularly vulnerable groups such as youth and the long-term unemployed have been abolished, and many people's incomes have dropped below the subsistence level. Because no rudimentary safety nets of any kind have been installed, the deregulation and flexibilization of labor markets and social security has led to an expansion of the low-wage sector, with one quarter of the population descending into mass poverty.

Meanwhile, developments in Greece have become a warning to the whole of Europe. Greece has been made a laboratory for a social experiment intended to clarify how far the system of working poverty – the exploitation of labor power below its subsistence level – can be taken and rendered permanent. The experiment is being extended to ever larger segments of the pauperized middle classes.

But the progressive, all-encompassing process of de-democratization has yielded effects the Bonapartist puppet regime did not expect. The dual system of clientelistic party dynasties no longer has a future. The major parties have pushed their own social base to the brink. Their leading exponents have resigned themselves to their resulting loss of popularity, on the assumption that the specific features of Greece's electoral system would continue to guarantee their dominant position. However, opinion polls conducted before 6 May 2012 showed that PASOK was gradually becoming a splinter party, due to its being justly blamed for implementation of the austerity programs. The decline of Nea Dimokratia has been slower to set in and less dramatic, since ND announced its support for the "memorandums" rather late. In April 2012, both parties still commanded about 35 percent of potential votes. This was just sufficient for the coalition government envisioned by the party leaders and the troika, given the fifty-seat bonus. However, a further loss of votes was likely, since many former PASOK and ND delegates who had been excluded from their parliamentary factions after failing to vote in accordance with the party line set about creating new political parties prior to the upcoming elections.

There were other examples of efforts to use the vacuum created by the Bonapartist transformation and begin moving in new directions. Every week, new political groups and ballot initiatives were set up. Transcending the clientelistic dual system, they proffered various solutions for overcoming the havoc wrought by the austerity programs. There was even talk of a new lease of life for the parliamentary left. According to opinion polls conducted in mid-March, the share of potential left-wing voters increased; it was estimated to lie somewhere in the vicinity of 35 percent. In light of the Greek electoral system's specific features, this increase – shared by the left-wing alliance SYRIZA, the moderate Democratic Left (the product of a June 2010 split within SYRIZA) and the Communist Party (KKE) – fueled hopes of a left-wing majority government. The formation of such a government would have presupposed that the three organizations unite and form a single governing party. While SYRIZA chairman Alexis Tsipras was strongly in favor of this option, the other two parties rejected it. Fotis Kouvelis, leader of the Democratic Left, and Aleka Papariga, KKE's general secretary, were both opposed to the proposal, for very different reasons.

All in all, the future seemed uncertain. As the social and economic decline continued, the political awakening prompted by the downfall of the party dynasties began to seem rather eerie. And there were too many unknown variables. For instance, nobody knew exactly how many voters would simply flout Greece's system of compulsory suffrage and refuse to cast their ballot. Growing political instability meant that further postponement of the election date was out of the question. During the second week of April, Papadimos' interim government finally set a date: 6 May 2012. Since the decline of the pro-austerity parties continued, the interim government assumed the first round of elections would fail to yield a government majority.[53] Like its multilateral mentors, it expected a second round of elections in June and hoped the revival of political dissent would subside by then, with the bulk of the population accepting the view that there was no change of course to be effected on the level of the political institutions. In this scenario, an extremely low voter turnout would allow the political forces willing to continue the austerity course to form a coalition government. There are plans to implement another austerity package as early as June 2012, including further budget cuts of 11 billion euros by 2014.

On 6 May, early elections were held. The voter turnout was rather low for Greece: just above 60 percent.[54] The coalition parties in favor of the troika program were punished even more harshly than expected: while ND's votes dropped below the 20-percent mark (to 18.9 percent), it remained the strongest party, with PASOK winning just 13.2 percent of the vote. In spite of the 50-seat bonus, this was not enough for an ND/PASOK governmental majority. On the left, SYRIZA made enormous electoral gains. With a 16.8 percent share of the vote, it was the second strongest parliamentary party, close on ND's heels and ahead of PASOK; KKE and the Democratic Left obtained 8.5 and 6.1

percent of the vote, respectively. The gains right-wing parties made at the expense of ND and the Laos Party (the latter dropped below the 3-percent mark) were also remarkable: the "Independent Greeks", an ND breakaway party, jumped to 10.6 percent, while the neo-fascist "Golden Dawn" obtained 7 percent of the vote. This unambiguous vote against austerity policies sealed the fate of Greece's two-party dynasty.

One day after the elections, the struggle to form a new government began, as stipulated by the constitution. First, ND party leader Samarás was appointed head of government, but he threw in the towel after a few hours. Next, it was the turn of SYRIZA chairman Tsipras, and finally of PASOK's party leader Venizelos. In contrast to Samarás, they made genuine efforts to build a majority coalition, but they failed as well. Another round of elections became inevitable.

The second round of elections was held in mid-May 2012 – under extreme circumstances. Many foreign companies had begun to close down their local subsidiaries. Major Greek shipping companies publicly discussed relocating their company headquarters, and small investors began to withdraw their money from the bank in order to hoard it or invest it in the "safe havens" Switzerland and Germany. These trends accelerated the deterioration of the Greek economy, which was further aggravated by expert statements on the results of Greece's possible exit or exclusion from the eurozone. There were predictions of a further 30 percent decline in GDP, rising unemployment (up to 34 percent) and a 40 percent inflation rate. It was also predicted that as a result of these developments, Greece would abruptly cease importing medical drugs, crude oil and food.

The pro-austerity parties that had lost the first round of elections invoked this nightmare scenario to deter voters from supporting their left-wing rivals. The Coalition of the Radical Left (SYRIZA) made it perfectly clear it did not wish to overturn the austerity measures at the price of leaving the eurozone.

Nevertheless, the eurozone's decision-making centers and media threatened to expel Greece if the left opposition won the elections. This threat benefited the parties responsible for the austerity policies. To most Greeks, the country's exit from the eurozone – and, ultimately, from the European Union – was and continues to be a nightmare scenario, and not just for economic reasons. An isolated Greece would once more become what Greece has repeatedly been throughout its history: a pawn in the game of the great powers, and one that ends up, sooner or later, as a dictatorship. So the Greeks were faced with a choice between retention of the austerity policies (in an attenuated form, at best) and a head-on confrontation that might lead to Berlin and Brussels expelling their country from Europe's institutions. Everything suggested the parties that had supported austerity would once more come out on top, all the more so as they promised to mitigate the harshest effects of the memoranda.

The second round of elections was held on 17 June 2012. Nea Dimokratia emerged as the strongest party, receiving 29.7 percent of the vote. Thanks to the 50-seat bonus, ND obtained 129 parliamentary seats. PASOK managed to more or less hold its ground, obtaining 33 seats, while the SYRIZA breakaway party Dimar (Democratic Left) obtained 20 seats. The Coalition of the Radical Left (SYRIZA) made substantial gains, commanding 27.9 percent of the vote (71 seats). Meanwhile, the Communist Party (KKE) received only half as many votes as during the first round of elections, thereby obtaining 12 parliamentary seats. Nothing stood in the way of a pro-austerity coalition government under ND party leader Antonis Samarás. It was only the distribution of power within the coalition that had changed: PASOK – and the Democratic Left – had become junior partners.

Three days after the elections, the three new governing parties signed a coalition agreement. They announced that they would renegotiate the austerity pact, but without putting Greece's eurozone membership at risk. This qualification made it clear from the outset that there would be only minor attenuations; the austerity measures would not be challenged fundamentally. Thus the course was set for resumption of the earlier restrictive policy, and SYRIZA announced that it would maintain its rigid oppositional stance. Key exponents of PASOK and the Democratic Left realized they would once more lose legitimacy among their followers. In order to contain the possible damage, they dispatched no delegates to the council of ministers. With the exception of the ministry of finance and three other ministries (the ministry of justice, the ministry of agriculture and the environmental ministry), all portfolios were assigned to ND delegates. These changes notwithstanding, the new government was a toned-down replica of the November 2011 technocratic government, only that this time it had been legitimated by a plebiscite. The executive director of the National Bank of Greece, Vassilis Rapanos, was chosen to be minister of finance, but before he was sworn in, he was replaced – putatively for health reasons – by Giannis Stournaras, a banker and economist. Stournaras represented the Greek bourgeoisie's last effort at collaboration. The new government's chances of survival will depend on the extent to which troika policymakers are prepared to attenuate their austerity diktat. A catalog of requested changes was presented to the troika just a few days after the formation of the government. The new government has asked that the 11 billion euros worth of additional budget cuts originally scheduled for late June be implemented more slowly, over a period of four years. In addition to this, the new government intends to discontinue mass layoffs in the public sector. It is also planning to raise the minimum wage and the minimum pension somewhat. The coming months will show to what extent the troika's decision-making bodies are prepared to settle for this agenda.

German Rigor and German History

So far, our background analysis of the Greek debt crisis has ignored an important protagonist. We wanted first to illustrate the interaction between Greece's political class, the country's multilateral creditors and their associated interest groups. To an extent, we have distanced ourselves from the prevailing tendency to reduce the conflicts about the so-called bailout package – the triad of austerity programs, debt cuts and loans – to a matter of Greek-German relations. Our aim was to set ourselves off from resentful discourses that substitute critical analysis with crude psychology. Nevertheless, the German ruling elites do play an important role in the multinational crisis intervention network constituted by the IMF, the European Central Bank, the European Commission and the Institute of International Finance. What is more, in the past two years even moderate and unprejudiced observers have repeatedly noted that policymakers and other protagonists from Germany have displayed not just unusual rigor but also a tendency to degrade and humiliate Greek society. How is this behavior to be accounted for? Is it a first manifestation of Germany's aspirations to the status of a great power? Does Germany mean to move beyond the political and economic hegemony it has enjoyed since the 1990s, by taking off the gloves in its dealings with other EU states?[55] Or should we assume that the trend towards German supremacy in Europe, actively promoted by Germany since the 1990s, has run its course now that crisis has come to Greece and the eurozone's other peripheral states? Let us finally try to clarify what cards Germany's ruling elites are playing in the poker game that is the Greek crisis, and why they are behaving so unrelentingly.

We have already addressed one reason for the overanxious manner in which Germany is playing its power game: what is at stake in Greece is the architecture of the entire European Union.

This architecture was created, in the main, by a group of ordoliberal financial economists associated with the German Federal Bank.[56] Two important preconditions were the annexation of East Germany and the subsequent *de facto* peace treaty between the government of "unified" Germany and the former allied forces. The monetary and fiscal experiences garnered during the annexation of East Germany were applied to the European Community in the form of the Maastricht convergence criteria. Moreover, the structures and institutions set up by the late 1990s gave highest macro-economic priority to deflationist monetary and price stability. The aim was to curb internal economic growth while improving the EU's international competitiveness; improvements in the latter were expected to manifest themselves in rising export quota and current account surpluses. Labor and social policy were fully subordinated to the economic objectives guiding monetary and fiscal policy. This was not difficult to achieve, as the practice of "strategic underemployment" associated with the restrictive monetary and price policies weakened the bargaining power of wage workers and favored a system of constant real wage declines and social cuts.

The introduction of a unified European currency, the euro, and the decision to exempt the European Central Bank from comprehensive economic and political control, granting it the kind of independence that is written into the statutes of the German Federal Bank, further bolstered the ordoliberal model of stability at the beginning of the new millennium. It could now be supplemented with a monetary replica of the gold standard system. Maximum price increases of two percent were stipulated as the "inflation target."

What is intriguing about the success story of how Germany became the main architect of European unification is that since introduction of the euro, the German elites have increasingly used the new currency to promote their own economic interests.[57] They developed a model that combines a continuous decline in real wages with a rise in labor productivity, the latter being induced mainly by technological means. Between 2001 and 2011, the average annual increase in nominal wages was 1.6 percent, but real wages declined by 4.2 percent during the same period. Meanwhile, labor productivity increased by 1.2 percent a year. The result was a steady decline in the ratio of the wage bill to domestic labor productivity, or unit labor costs. Since unit labor costs are more closely correlated with the price structure than the money supply or government debt, the Germans were able to use wage dumping, which is also highly profitable for companies, to systematically lower export prices. At the beginning of the crisis, labor unit costs in Greece and the EU's other peripheral states were 30 percent higher than in Germany; by the time the austerity programs were implemented, they were 35 percent higher. There is a close correlation between this labor cost differential and export prices, so that the German policy of intra-European wage and price dumping was the most important factor in the decline of the Greek economy, all the more so as the de facto gold standard precluded monetary countermeasures. To be sure, "home-made" factors also played a crucial role: witness Greece's excessive capital imports after the country's admission to the eurozone and the extravagant price increases they entailed. However, the main cause of the malaise was the German economic elite's destabilization of the European Union. Effected by wage and price dumping after the introduction of the euro, this destabilization ruined the economically weaker peripheral states. We may assume that Germany's ruling and functional elites gradually became aware of these causalities, even though ordoliberal monetary and price theory denies the priority of labor unit costs for the development of prices. But as long as they are not prepared to challenge their own regulatory narrow-mindedness, they are faced with only two options: either they will have to kick all national economies that have become "asymmetrical" out of the eurozone one by one, so at the end they will be left on their own, or they will have to use Greece's extreme over-indebtedness to force the Greek economy to remedy the imbalance by adjusting itself radically to Germany's low-wage strategy. So far, they have chosen the second option.

It would be wrong, however, to attribute the Germans' hubris only to their ordoliberal narrow-mindedness. Socio-psychological reasons also play a part. German-Greek relations are fraught with historical burdens. They have been since the Second World War. In April 1941, the Germans attacked and occupied Greece. They cooperated with the axis powers Italy and Bulgaria in dividing Greece into three occupation zones, and then systematically ransacked the country.[58] Immediately after the invasion, they confiscated all strategically important raw materials and transported them to the Reich. They then brought the coal and steel industries under their control and exploited them systematically. At the same time, they depreciated the national currency – the drachma – and established unequal exchange rates as part of a bilateral clearing system. On top of that, they extorted immense amounts of money and forced loans from the National Bank in order to finance the costs of the occupation, as well as gargantuan investments in military infrastructure. These *Raubwirtschaft* measures triggered hyperinflation; as early as the winter of 1941/42, soaring food prices led to a hunger catastrophe that left 100,000 dead. What followed was the ransacking and destruction of more than 1,600 towns as part of anti-partisan warfare in 1942/43, leading to one million homeless. In addition, when the German occupants retreated from Greece in the fall of 1944, they destroyed most of the economic and transportation infrastructure. In this way, Greece shared the fate of the occupied territories in Eastern Europe, whose socio-economic foundations fell prey to unprecedented predatory and extermination warfare.

In January 1946, an allied conference on reparations adjudicated Greece a compensation that amounted to 3.5 percent of the total sum of German reparations: 7.1 billion US dollars at 1938 prices.[59] Greece became one of the 18 recipients of German reparations. A small part of this amount was paid in the early postwar period, another in 1960. But the German legal successors of the "Third Reich" never paid the bulk of the debt. Since the 1946 Paris treaty on reparations was never annulled, the legal successors of the *Raubwirtschaft* institutions active in Greece are still in debt to the Greek economy: the German Central Bank, the Federation of German Industry, the Federation of German Wholesale, Foreign Trade and Services, Deutsche Bank, Siemens, Rheinmetall, ThyssenKrupp, Degussa and the German tobacco industry. Even if we ignore accrued and compound interest since 1946 and take into account that the US dollar's purchasing power has declined by a factor of 15 since 1938, German total debt still amounts to 79 billion euros.

These liabilities were unambiguously determined in accordance with international law. So how did the Germans manage to avoid payment? How have they been able to behave as they have during Greece's current debt crisis, in spite of this historical legacy? The German economy is itself the worst "debt transgressor" in the history of modern finance. To this day, and in spite of changing historical circumstances, its financial and monetary policymakers have succeeded in minimizing their debt payments and outmaneuvering their private and public creditors.[60] Who is to make them behave differently when dealing with the powerless representatives of Greece's relatively small economy?

After the First World War, the Germans were forced to consent to massive reparation payments as part of the Treaty of Versailles. Since then, circumventing these liabilities or reducing them to a minimum has been an important goal of Germany's economic, financial, and foreign policies as developed by the country's elites. Initially, these elites attempted to eliminate their reparation debt by a strategy of deliberate hyperinflation. When that approach failed in the fall of 1923, they enacted a currency reform and reached an agreement with their Entente creditors: Germany would henceforth issue international bonds to refinance its yearly payments. In 1929/30, as part of a first generous debt cut, these bonds were converted into new bonds with far lower interest rates and redemption sums. Then came the world economic crisis and the transition from the Weimar Republic to Heinrich Brüning's presidential dictatorship. Brüning and his financial advisers saw an opportunity to get rid of reparation debt by means of a deflationary austerity policy. As a result, international creditors began to have doubts about Germany's payment morale and withdrew their loans from the country, thereby causing the collapse of its banking system. Now Germany was genuinely insolvent. The plans of the national financial oligarchy that worked in the shadow of the presidential cabinets seemed to be coming to fruition. In July of 1931, US president Hoover announced a one-year debt moratorium, and in 1932 the remaining reparation payments were reduced from 110 billion reichsmarks to 3 billion goldmarks. But even this remainder was not claimed by anyone.

Interest did continue to accrue on the German bonds that had been issued on the basis of reparation liabilities. But in 1934, the National Socialist government stopped paying this interest, later signing a "standstill agreement" with international creditors that was renewed annually. More than anyone else, banker Hermann J. Abs made a name for himself on this occasion. Abs began his career as co-owner of a renowned private bank; by 1938, he was head of Deutsche Bank AG's foreign department.

Then came the Second World War. Like the First World War, it was begun and lost by Germany. As long as the victorious coalition of Germany's enemies remained more or less intact, Germany's prospects of avoiding new reparations were dim. The Soviet occupation zone and East Germany were made to pay significant reparations until 1953, when Moscow waived all outstanding claims. The reparation agreement signed in Paris in January 1946 concerned the western occupation zones, which later became West Germany. The Inter-Allied Reparation Agency was set up and given access to German foreign assets. The Agency ordered the partial dismantling of German heavy industry and a stop to arms production. In the early 1950s, these measures were tacitly discontinued, as the Cold War – which had by that point become "hot" in Korea – made the Anglo-American victors review their priorities. The German ruling elites and the socio-economic potential they commanded were now badly needed to bolster the economic potential of the "free West."

The confrontation between East and West gave the West German elites a higher status, and they were well aware of this. They perceived an opportunity both to get rid of the reparations imposed on them in 1946 and to minimize the amount of interest payable on the Weimar reparation bonds issued under the 1932 Treaty of Lausanne. Debt restructuring negotiations began in London in early 1953. On both sides of the table, old acquaintances from the post-1934 "standstill negotiations" met again. Both prewar debt and about 15 billion deutschmarks worth of debt accumulated by the western occupation zones during the first years of the postwar period (occupation costs and Marshall Plan loans) were up for negotiation.

The West German negotiators, headed by Hermann J. Abs, benefited from the goodwill of the Anglo-American powers, especially the USA. And their approach paid off.[61] At the very beginning of the negotiations, the international creditors – including Greece – waived their claims to 14 billion deutschmarks worth of compound interest payments that had been outstanding since 1934. The amount of prewar debt to be negotiated was thereby reduced to 13.5 billion deutschmarks. Next, it was decided not to use the gold standard as the basis for the negotiations, resulting in a further reduction of the prewar debt to 9.6 billion deutschmarks.

Later in the negotiations, the creditors also accepted reduced interest rates and the waiving of compound interest. Finally, 7.3 billion deutschmarks remained. Since the postwar debt was reduced to less than 7 billion deutschmarks, total claims amounted to 14 billion deutschmarks. The repayment was scheduled for a period of 20 to 35 years, in order not to jeopardize West Germany's economic growth. Thus real debt was cut by more than two thirds. The total amount came to a mere 20 percent of West German GDP (70 billion deutschmarks in 1953); on average, its repayment (interest included) claimed 3.5 percent of German export earnings. Today, the representatives of the crisis-shaken Greek economy can only dream of such generous conditions – granted, moreover, to a rapidly growing economic power.

In addition, the servicing of the reparation debts determined in the 1946 Treaty of Paris was postponed until the signing of a peace treaty. A (surrogate) peace treaty did eventually take effect as a result of the so-called "Two Plus Four" negotiations in 1990. However, reparation debt was never mentioned during these negotiations. The West German elites had accomplished what their predecessors in the 1920s and 1930s had striven for: near total debt relief.

Thus, in the course of the 20th century, the German ruling elites have twice managed to evade the economic consequences of world wars they were responsible for. No exact aggregate figure is available to date, but we can assume that the representatives of the 20th century's worst public debt transgressor have repaid no more than ten percent of their debt and interest liabilities. They thereby created financial and economic conditions that were essential to the West German economic miracle of the 1950s and 1960s. As the West German elites reforged their economic hegemony, the national economies they had ransacked and ruined were left to take care of themselves. The reparation waiver imposed on these economies seriously hampered their restart and led to a structural asymmetry that was increased further by the Germans during the European integration process.

The Germans would have been well advised to exercise restraint during the negotiations on the management of the Greek debt crisis. They are living in a glass house, and yet they insist on the comparatively small Greek economy repaying its debt at virtually any cost. It is high time to put a stop to the hubris of Germany's ruling elites and the multilateral institutions supporting them. As the ancient philosopher Heraclitus of Ephesus already knew: hubris needs putting out, even more than a house on fire.

The Problem of an Alternative

Those masterminding and imposing austerity policies tend to describe their decisions as responses to given constraints, implying that there is no alternative. In the European Union's core states in particular, they are resolutely seconded by the media. The result is a far-reaching paralysis of critical thought that has already worked its way far into the left, reinforcing the tendency to resort to historically outdated models when searching for counter-perspectives, and thus to overlook alternatives that emerge from within processes of social resistance. In conclusion, we will try to bridge this divide. We will describe alternatives inherent in the system, and then point out perspectives that go beyond it. The following considerations are mainly based on current discussions within the Greek left.

System-Inherent Approaches

We have already described the dilemma the newly elected PASOK government faced in the fall of 2009. The economic boom had rested mainly on capital imports, and the public refinancing operations driving it had already gotten out of hand before they were rendered altogether impossible by a recession that lasted more than a year. Since resorting to depreciation was out of the question, the Papandreou government was left with only two practical options: it could either accept the Trojan horse of multilateral credits or declare itself insolvent. We know what decision was taken and have familiarized ourselves with the consequences. But what would have happened if the second option had been chosen? The answer is simple and in some ways surprising.

By declaring national bankruptcy and thus implementing a debt moratorium, the protagonists of the Greek economy would have gained a lot more room for maneuver. Firstly, they could have used the funds freed up by discontinued loan and interest payments to finance an anti-cyclical stimulus program with a volume corresponding to about six percent of Greece's annual GDP. Secondly, they would have presented the European institutions with a fait accompli. EU treaties feature neither exclusion criteria for "refractory" member states nor rules on how to handle national bankruptcies. Therefore, the European Commission and the European Central Bank would have had to reach an agreement with the Greek government in order to prevent the debt crisis from spreading through the region. This would have created new options for the Papandreou government, such as a legal procedure for waiving large parts of government debt and converting the remaining debt into eurobonds. Thirdly, these and other measures would have won time that could have been used to reduce the economic shock effects created by a national bankruptcy. Above all, like the Argentinian government in the years after 2001, the Papandreou government would have retained control of its debt restructuring and consolidation process – without having to withdraw from the eurozone or even the European Union. The EU bodies would likely have refrained from pressuring Greece to leave the eurozone, as the reintroduction of the drachma and the resulting hyperinflation would have forced them to write off their loans, which are denominated in euros. The conclusion is clear: national bankruptcy would have prevented further aggravation of the crisis; it would have accelerated economic consolidation and saved Greek society from long-term pauperization. Seen from a global perspective, the Greek debt crisis is a rather marginal event, so the global effects would have been limited – although investors would no doubt have suffered substantial losses.

After a full two years of austerity policies, the macroeconomic alternatives have changed fundamentally. Greece's deindustrialization and pauperization processes have progressed considerably, making the adoption of countermeasures both more difficult and more urgent. The representatives of Greece's Coalition of the Radical Left (SYRIZA) have understood this, and they have allowed themselves to be inspired by the widespread demand for plausible alternatives.[62] In their programmatic declarations on the occasion of the 6 May elections, they called for a debt moratorium, the transformation of austerity and debt restructuring agreements into social and growth-enhancing programs and a partial waiving of government debt. This set of macro-economic measures is designed to halt the rampant redistribution of income from the lower to the upper echelons of society while restoring social and economic justice and beginning to rebuild the Greek economy in an environmentally sustainable way. According to SYRIZA, such a change of course is only possible within a European context and should be combined with a comprehensive regional disarmament program. Thus SYRIZA aims for an economic and fiscal policy shift on the European level.

This model includes important parameters for the correction and reversal of the overall socio-economic trend. However, it lacks some important elements which would have given it more bite – elements quite compatible, incidentally, with a left Keynesian reformist perspective. In my view, the rightfully demanded debt moratorium should have been combined with an exact figure on the amount of debt to be annulled; 80 percent of aggregate real debt would be appropriate.[63] Secondly, there are no detailed proposals on how to reverse the asymmetric process of economic redistribution; measures might include raising business and property taxes and confiscating all assets that have been transferred abroad. Thirdly, it is important to call for the conversion of all current troika loans into interest-free European reconstruction bonds; payment of the German reparation debt – a "lost subsidy" – would have to be a central component of this. This is the point at which one can see most clearly that SYRIZA's electoral platform is not sufficiently rooted in a firmly "euro-socialist" perspective. This may seem understandable, considering the current weakness of European left Keynesianism. But since SYRIZA's project explicitly embraces the European integration of Greece, the mechanisms by which to effect a Europe-wide homogenization and democratization of labor, social, fiscal and economic policy should be clearly identified and enshrined as "future values."

What is to be Done? Perspectives from Below

But there are also approaches that are situated outside given systemic structures, either because they display an explicitly anti-systemic orientation or because they are informed by a vision of life that rests on an alternative conception of economics. For those committed to such extra-systemic approaches, Greece has also become a laboratory: persons facing extreme processes of expropriation and pauperization have to make existential decisions that may challenge habitual norms and lead in all sorts of directions.

The Communist Party of Greece (KKE) also advocates an anti-systemic political approach. Since its last (2009) party congress, however, it has openly endorsed the legacy of Stalinism.[64] It has thereby lost the support of virtually all intellectuals. Nevertheless, under the leadership of general secretary Aleka Papariga, this active cadre party, which is rooted in important parts of the working class, has developed a political program that represents a kind of a renaissance of the Bolshevik revolutionary doctrine. In accordance with this doctrine, the KKE is placing its hopes in a popular uprising against the crisis policies of the Greek ruling elites. Its cadres will then seize political power and establish a dictatorship of the proletariat. Acting as the vanguard of the masses, they will nationalize banks and enforce Greece's withdrawal from the eurozone, the European Union and NATO. They will set up a centralized planning system that is geared to rapid productivity increases and allocates labor power and economic ressources to strategic sectors. In this way, the presently weakest link in the chain of European imperialism will stabilize itself and initiate the restoration of proletarian internationalism. It goes without saying that such programmatic commitments do not allow for alliances with other left-wing currents and parties. KKE participates in elections mainly for propagandistic reasons and with an eye to destabilizing the two-party oligarchy.

The party platform reads like a bottle message bearing witness to the faded certainties of the Boshevik variant of social democracy. Nonetheless, its proponents can count on the support of some parts of the Greek underclasses, so we should take it seriously, in spite of the burdensome historical legacy associated with it. What would happen if a popular uprising allowed the KKE to "storm the Winter Palace" and seize political power?

In light of the party platform, the answer is clear: the KKE and its associated union and mass organizations would set up a kind of "war communist" dictatorship. This dictatorship would collapse within just a few months, even without military interventions from within and/or outside Greece, if only because of its nation-state orientation. Initially, there would be large-scale capital flight, which it would not be possible to prevent by nationalizing foreign trade and closing the borders. As a result, banks and insurance companies would have to be nationalized and their vaults and accounts would be emptied. Even a currency reform reintroducing the drachma would drag on for a long time, due to the communist cadres' incompetence, and the inevitable process of hyperinflation would thereby be rendered ungovernable. In addition, immediate European sanctions would paralyze key sectors of the Greek economy. All attempts to introduce a centralized planning system would thus prove futile. Moreover, the system's dirigiste claim to leadership of the direct producers would rapidly prompt an irresolvable conflict between the communist party become workers' government and the working class. The project of communist transition would soon collapse in a vortex of mass impoverishment, hunger catastrophes and repression. The victorious powers' historians would ultimately conclude that while Greek society was pushed to the brink by the troika's austerity programs, it was the communists who gave it the final shove.

A credible and promising perspective from below should therefore be transnational, anti-statist and based on grassroots democracy.

A transnational perspective is vital given today's well-developed cross-border economic and social networks. Geographically, socio-economically and politically, Greece is part of several regions: it belongs to the Mediterranean region and to southeastern and southern Europe as well as to the European Union and the eurozone. A perspective that transcends the current system can only be developed if these overlapping regions are taken into account. Greek resistance to the austerity programs must build ties to the social mass movements within the various regions. For instance, the demilitarization of Greece and the entire region can only be accomplished through close cooperation with the social movements in neighboring Mediterranean states, Turkey in particular. To overcome the unit labor cost asymmetry between the core states of the European Union and the EU periphery, the Greek social resistance needs to collaborate with new mass initiatives from the core states: initiatives that attack wage dumping on all levels[65] and end the rule of the European gold standard. These two examples may suffice. They show that the main issues of left Keynesian reform – discussed above by reference to the SYRIZA platform – can only be resolved across Europe by operating within such transnational contexts. The pivotal elements of such a transformation perspective can at least be suggested here: equalization of working conditions, mass incomes and social standards as a first step towards the abolition of commanded labor; expropriation of major capital assets through surcharges on capital and progressive taxation; cancellation of all debt; establishment of a fiscal compensation fund and a macro-economic framework for satisfying the needs of the masses; abolition of the military-industrial complexes and apparatuses of repression; the secularization of what are de facto state churches.

To be sure, other regional networks, such as those encompassing social movements from the Maghreb or the Near East, will set other priorities – we need think only of the abolition of the Schengen Treaty and the integration of mass migration. Consequently, the social transformation will not be limited to the European power bloc; it will also have a transcontinental and global dimension. An alliance with the world-wide "Occupy Movement" might also be considered. For more than a year, it has symbolically encircled the world system's nerve centers and centers of power, undermining their legitimacy, and it has now also become aware of the "social question," which has been aggravated by the global crisis. Its European offshoot, the "Bloccupy Frankfurt" movement, has focused its critical attention on the European Central Bank and might also play an important role.

The fixation on the state and the authoritarian-productivist habitus of the traditional left and its revolutionary theory are obsolete. Departing for new horizons has become easier because the social strata that are the bearers of transnational mass movements have developed new visions of life that are no longer subjugated to the practical constraints of everyday life under capitalism. All regions within the transnational network have featured alternative economy projects for some time now. Given the dynamic process of impoverishment the crisis has produced, the importance of these projects – farming communes, handicraft cooperatives, tenant and housing cooperatives, artistic communes, health collectives and communities of care – has increased considerably. They provide impulses for a youth that has been denied its future prospects, as well as for the pauperized underclasses of the urban agglomerations. In Greece as elsewhere, they are increasingly perceived as offering an alternative to emigration, the proletariat's classic response to acute pauperization. For the working class, mutual support has always been an elementary principle of survival. In Greece, it might serve as a stimulus for the restoration of solidarity and social equality.

Left to themselves, these initiatives are not capable of escaping poverty and the scarcity that dominates their barter economies. This will remain the case unless they merge with movements for the social (re-)appropriation of public goods whose spectrum of activity ranges from the occupation of buildings and neighborhoods to the reappropriation of municipal enterprises, public transportation and public services, in addition to the symbolic processes of reappropriation seen during general strikes and factory occupations. To the extent that such temporary stoppages of the capitalist process of reproduction and reproduction can be rendered permanent and combined with the appropriation of a self-determined society's material necessities of life, a transnationally coordinated systemic rupture has some prospects of success.

Moreover, the topography of alternative economy and social reappropriation opens up genuine spaces of direct democracy.[66] The expansion of these spaces allows ever larger sections and strata of the subaltern classes to participate in learning processes that enable them to begin moving towards a social life that is self-determined, egalitarian and based on direct democracy. This will make it possible to overcome the Bonapartist combinations of deformed nation-statehood and European technocracy, thus initiating a new era of direct democracy.

All in all, we can distinguish two complementary aspects of the overarching effort to superate the current system: transnational coordination of social, economic and political transformation, and its locally rooted social foundations as shaped by the triad of alternative economy, direct democracy and reappropriation. These two poles form a dialectical whole, although their unity does not constitute itself spontaneously; it needs rather to be actively created. In my opinion, it is necessary to set up an international association that establishes the link between emergent local processes of self-determination and transnational objectives. This international association needs to be democratically constituted and capable of continuously internalizing the learning processes of the social mass movements. Once the mass initiatives have reached a certain degree of stability, they should develop a rotational system of delegation that preserves the international association's democratic grounding and precludes tendencies towards the autonomization of the bureaucracy.

Time to Act

For decades, the defeats suffered by the left's various currents have stalled our theoretical and practical endeavours. We have done well to examine the underlying authoritarian aberrations, analytic deficits and false certainties.[67]

Now, however, it is time to set out for new shores. The paradigmatic starting point is the Greek crisis, in which the multilaterally active ruling classes are preparing to ruin an entire society. They are using a relatively small national economy to determine to what extent the subaltern classes – and no one else, ideally – can be forced to pay the costs of the crisis, which have been transferred to the state budget. In doing so, Greece's ruling elites and the protagonists of the troika are willing to hazard not just mass impoverishment but the collapse of an entire society. If this experiment is successful, we will be faced with a new stage of exploitation the world over.

We cannot simply stand back and watch these practices of the ruling elites, for they are accelerating the capitalist social formation's inherent tendency toward self-destruction. We urgently need to halt this development and confront the masterminds and agents of the austerity programs with a plausible alternative.

Greece in the Crisis: Basic Macro-Economic Data

(Real changes in relation to the previous year are given in percent, unless stated otherwise.)

Year	2007	2008	2009	2010	2011	2012[1]	2013[1]	2014[1]
Nominal GDP (billion euros)	223	233	232	227	217	216	216,4	217
Real GDP (percent)	3,0	-0,1	-3,3	-3,5	-6,9	-4,7	0,9	2,3
Private consumption (percent)	3,8	4,0	-2,3	-3,6	-7,0	-4,7	-1,4	0,7
Unemployment rate (percent)	8,3	7,7	9,4	12,5	17,0	19,0	19,5	18,8
Consumer prices (percent)	2,9	4,1	1,2	4,7	3,1	0,8	0,9	1,0
Labor unit costs (percent)				-0,4	-1,0	-7,8	-1,3	-1,9
Labor productivity (percent)[2]	3,8	1,5	-1,5	-2,0	-4,2	-1,3		
Balance of payments (billion euros)	32,6	-34,7	-25,8	-23,0	-18,2	-13,4	-11,7	-9,0
Balance of payments (percent of GDP)	-14,6	-14,9	-11,1	-10,1	-10,3	-6,9	-5,3	-4,6
Government revenue (billion euros)			87,7	89,9	87,9	90,0	91,6	94,6
Government spending (billion euros)			111,8	101,3	92,8	89,5	86,5	83,2
Balance of primary budget (billion euros)			-24,1	-11,4	-4,9	0,5	5,1	11,4

Year	2007	2008	2009	2010	2011	2012[1]	2013[1]	2014[1]
Primary balance of state budget (percent of GDP)[3]	-2,0	-4,9	-10,4	-5,0	-2,4	-1,0	1,8	4,5
Interest rate on government bonds (billion euros)			12,3	12,6	14,7	10,4	10,6	10,5
Aggregate balance of state budget (billion euros)			-36,4	-24,0	-19,6	-10,9	-8,3	-3,2
Gross government debt (billion euros)			299	329	351	376 271[4]	354,9	349,4
Gross government debt (percent of GDP)	107	111	129	145	165	160	164	161
Rate of return on ten-year government bonds (percent)	9,6	10,1	13,2	12,5	19,7	25,4		
Market value of government bonds[5]	102	95	86	45	32	26		
Interest rate on government debt I (percent of GDP)			5,3	5,5	6,8	4,8	4,8	4,8
Interest rate on government debt II (percent of government revenue)			14,0	14,0	14,4	11,6	11,6	11,1

1 IMF/European Commission forecast.

2 Expenditure of human labor per defined amount of goods/net product.

3 Balance before interest return on government bonds.

4 Before and after the debt cut in March 2012.

5 In percent of nominal value (estimation based on media reports).

Sources:

Evaluation reports of the troika commission, 2011 and 2012

December 2011 IMF report, European Commission

Endnotes

1 The European Monetary System consisted of a currency basket that included the major currencies of the European Community (ECU) and limited the range of exchange rate fluctuations.

2 The Maastricht Treaty fixes the upper limit of total public debt at 60 percent of GDP; the upper limit of annual new debt is fixed at 3 percent of GDP.

3 On the Greek reparation and compensation claims arising from the Second World War, see Karl Heinz Roth, 'Die offene Reparationsfrage. Die Profiteure des Raubzugs müssen zahlen!', lunapark 21, no. 15 (fall 2011), pp. 51–55.

4 Cf. Winfried Wolf, 'Dritter Staatsbankrott? Griechische Schulden, deutsche Panzer, Euro-Diktat und eine Fakelaki-Ökonomie made by Siemens', undated manuscript (2010), p. 7.

5 Despite the enormous amount of resources mobilized, Siemens was left empty-handed: today, OTE is controlled by Deutsche Telekom.

6 Cf. Winfried Wolf, op. cit., p. 8.

7 These and the following figures are taken from the ongoing monitoring reports published by the European Commission, Eurostat and the European Central Bank, as well as from the website of the Greek Ministry of Finance.

8 Compare the reports published by Frankfurter Allgemeine Zeitung, Handelsblatt, the International Herald Tribune, Neue Zürcher Zeitung and The Economist since the spring of 2010.

9 Main Results of the Joint Monitoring of Greece by the European Commission, the European Central Bank and the International Monetary Fund (3 May–2 June 2011), 8 June 2011, henceforth cited according to a rough translation

prepared for the Federal Ministry of Finance.

10 Taking the May 2010 market value of Greek government bonds as a basis, this debt relief amounted to about 7 percent of total debt. On the actual volume of the debt relief envisioned in the debt restructuring negotiations that have taken place since 2010, see the interim conclusion below.

11 Headed by German top official Horst Reichenbach, the European Commission's task force began its work in the fall of 2011; in the months that followed, its staff was increased to include 45 experts.

12 Cf. Main Results, op. cit., Appendix 2: Preliminary Privatization Plan, pp. 14 f.

13 Cf. ibid., Table 3, p. 4.

14 Initially, the European Commission envisioned a total volume of 780 billion euros, but pressure from the German federal government and the German Central Bank led to this sum being reduced to 440 billion euros.

15 In the German press in particular, the Greek government was accused of sabotaging the comprehensive privatization program that had been agreed upon on 21 July. There was certainly some resistance to the program within the Greek administrative apparatus. In light of the rapidly declining value of Greek assets, privatizing them at this point in time would have amounted to a crash-price clearout sale.

16 This third set of loans replaced the second set (109 billions euros), which had been disbursed in July of 2011.

17 On 28 October 1940, fascist Italy confronted Greece with an ultimatum demanding permission to move its troops through the country and establish encampments on strategically important islands. Greece's response was an unambiguous "*Ochi*" ("No"). A few days later, Italy invaded Greece by crossing into the south of the country from Albania.

18 Nevertheless, the sixth instalment was not disbursed until

mid-December.

19 Papadimos is said to have played a major role in the statistical whitewash thanks to which Greece was admitted to the eurozone in spite of its flagrant violation of the criteria stipulated in the Maastricht Treaty.

20 Only family allowances and educational allowances for children attending professional schools and universities were retained. In effect, the average monthly wage of a hotel employee was reduced from 1,375 euros to 962 euros.

21 The same fate was suffered by two Laos delegates who had shown up at the parliamentary meeting and voted in favor of the austerity package.

22 Source: Bank of America, data summarized in graph accompanying the article 'Letzte Mahnung an Griechenland', Frankfurter Rundschau, 6 February 2012, p. 6.

23 The IIF was founded by 38 banks from the triad region in 1983, with the purpose of promoting the interests of these banks in the debt crisis of the early 1980s. To this day, it is the only globally networked coordination and lobbying center the financial corporations dispose of. Its executive board comprises 30 members and has been headed by Josef Ackermann since 2003.

24 'Schulden außer Kontrolle: Troika stellt Griechenland katastrophales Zeugnis aus', Spiegel Online, 17 February 2012.

25 'Griechenland-Krise: Bundesbank verweigert Teilnahme am Schuldenschnitt', Welt Online, 15 February 2012.

26 The board of the European Central Bank justified this measure by reference to the fact that the rating agency Standard & Poor's had spoken of a "selective default" on the part of Greece following the debt cut arranged with Greece's creditors. Cf. 'Die EZB akzeptiert keine Titel aus Griechenland als Pfand', Neue Zürcher Zeitung, 29. February 2012, p. 7; 'E.C.B. seeks to reassure markets on Greek debt', International Herald Tribune, 29 February 2012,

p. 15.

27 Eric Bonse, 'Diktat statt Hilfe', tageszeitung, 22 February 2012, p. 1.

28 'Sparen in Griechenland. Gesetze im Eilverfahren', Neue Zürcher Zeitung, 2 March 2012, p. 9.

29 Draghi had already disbursed 490 billion euros in December of 2011, in order to overcome the deadlock reached in the debt restructuring negotiations and make it easier for the other countries of the eurozone's periphery to obtain credit on the free bond markets.

30 This would have meant that credit default swaps with a net worth of more than 3 billion US dollars would have become payable.

31 The small group of creditors who rejected the debt restructuring agreement was included in the proceedings by means of a collective action clause.

32 Cf. Gregor Kritidis, 'Krise als Katalysator. Zur Transformation der griechischen Arbeiterbewegung', Sozial.Geschichte Online, 3 (2010), pp. 133–147; 'Griechenland: Einheit und Spaltung', Wildcat, 91 (2011), pp. 16–19.

33 On this and the following, see Noelle Burgi, 'Griechische Zustände', Le Monde Diplomatique, December 2011, p. 6; Alexander Kentikekenia et al., 'Health effects of financial crisis: omens of a Greek tragedy', The Lancet, 378 (2011), 9801, pp. 1457–1458.

34 'Verlust der EFG International. Hohe Restrukturierungskosten und Goodwill-Abschreibungen', Neue Zürcher Zeitung, 2 March 2012, p. 13.

35 'Geld oder Gericht. Griechenland will erstmals bei einem Unternehmer durchgreifen', Süddeutsche Zeitung, 9 March 2012, p. 19.

36 When Greek social scientist Zissis Papadimitriou recently called for the forcible repatriation of the capital assets that

have been transferred abroad, he provoked a storm of indignation.

37 For details see Karl-Heinz Roth, Die globale Krise, Hamburg: VSA, 2009, Chapter 3, pp. 62 ff.

38 This is the position of Detlef Hartmann and John Malamatinas, Krisenlabor Griechenland. Finanzmärkte, Kämpfe und die Neuordnung Europas, Berlin/Hamburg: Assoziation A, 2010.

39 Carlo Cottarelli/Lorenzo Forni/Jan Gottschalk/Paolo Mauro, Default in Today's Advanced Economies: Unnecessary, Undesirable, and Unlikely, Washington: International Monetary Fund, Fiscal Affairs Department, 1 September 2010.

40 On this and the following see Main Results, op. cit.; International Monetary Fund, Greece: Debt Stability Analysis, Strictly Confidential, 21 October 2011; International Monetary Fund, Greece: Fifth Review Under the Stand-By Arrangement, IMF Country Report no. 11/351, December 2011.

41 For instance, Carlo Cottarelli, director of the Fiscal Affair Department since 2008, won his spurs at the IMF overseeing structural adjustment programs in Albania, Croatia, Hungary, Serbia, Turkey and Russia. Poul Thomsen, head of the IMF team in Athens and vice director of the European Department, has been an IMF controller since 1987 and has dealt with countries including Yugoslavia, Slovenia and Romania. He led the IMF's Russia Department between 1998 and 2000, subsequently presiding over the IMF office in Moscow.

42 See Bergljot Barkbu/Barry Eichengreen/Ashoka Mody, 'International Financial Crises and the Multilateral Response: What the Historical Record Shows', Cambridge, MA: National Bureau of Economic Research, Working Paper 17361, August 2011.

43 See Otmar Issing, Der Euro. Geburt – Erfolg – Zukunft, Munich: Franz Vahlen, 2008, pp. 47 ff.
44 For more on Brüning, see page ## (translator's note).
45 Public sector workers' thirteenth and fourteenth monthly wage payments were abolished, the pension age was raised by two years and wage and hiring freezes were imposed within the public sector.
46 See Main Results, op. cit., Appendix 1: Additional Consolidation Measures for 2011 and Medium-Term Budget Strategy for 2012–2015.
47 See the previous footnote.
48 On this and the following, see 'Greece PCI Discussion', in: International Monetary Fund, Greece: Fifth Review Under the Stand-By Arrangement, pp. 10 ff., 36.
49 International Monetary Fund, Greece: Debt Sustainability Analysis, October 2011, pp. 2 ff., 7.
50 See for instance 'What to do about Greece', The Economist, 28 January 2012, pp. 9 ff.
51 On this and the following, see Gustav Auernheimer, 'Griechenland: Wahlschlacht im Schuldturm', Blätter für deutsche und internationale Politik, 57 (2012), 4, pp. 16–19.
52 On this and the following, see Zoe Lanara, 'Die Krise und die Schwächung der ArbeitnehmerInnen in Griechenland', Gegenblende, 16 November 2011, [www. gegenblende .de/12-2011].
53 See Nikki Kitsantonis, 'Greek leader sets stage for heated vote on May 6', International Herald Tribune, 12 April 2012, p. 3.
54 On this and the following, see the reports published in Athens News, Kathimerini Online (English edition), the International Herald Tribune and Neue Zürcher Zeitung from 8 May 2012 onward.
55 See for instance Jürg Dedial, 'Zahlmeister im Zugzwang', Neue Zürcher Zeitung, 17/18 March 2012, p. 1.

56 This emerges from these economists' own publications on the history of the plans underpinning the European unification process. See in particular Otmar Issing, Der Euro, op. cit.; Otmar Issing et al., Monetary Policy in the Euro Area: Strategy and Decision-Making in the European Central Bank, Cambridge: Cambridge University Press, 2001; Otmar Issing/Klaus Masuch, 'EWS, Währungsunion und Kapitalallokation. Neue Perspektiven durch die deutsche Wiedervereinigung', in: Claus Köhler/Rüdiger Pohl (ed.), Währungspolitische Probleme im integrierten Europa, Berlin: Duncker & Humblot, 1992, pp. 37–61.

57 On this and the following, see Heiner Flassbeck/Friederike Spiecker, 'Die deutsche Lohnpolitik sprengt die Europäische Währungsunion', WSI Mitteilungen, 58 (2005), 12, pp. 707–713; Heiner Flassbeck/Friederike Spiecker, Das Ende der Massenarbeitslosigkeit, Frankfurt on the Main: Westend, 2007; Heiner Flassbeck, Zehn Mythen der Krise, Frankfurt on the Main: Suhrkamp, 2012.

58 On this and the following, see Karl Heinz Roth, 'Kahlfraß, Nicht nur „ein paar niedergebrannte Ortschaften" – Die Zerstörung der griechischen Volkswirtschaft während der deutschen Besatzung 1941–1944', lunapark 21, 15 (2011), pp. 42–50.

59 On this and the following, see Karl Heinz Roth, 'Die offene Reparationsfrage', op. cit.

60 These facts have mainly been established by Albrecht Ritschl (London School of Economics). See Albrecht Ritschl, 'Deutschland ist der größte Schuldensünder des 20. Jahrhunderts', Spiegel Online, 21 June 2011; id., 'Athen auf dem Weg zu Weimarer Verhältnissen. Albrecht Ritschl im Gespräch mit Katrin Heise', Deutschlandradio Kultur, 14 June 2011.

61 On the following, see Christoph Buchheim, 'Das Londoner Schuldenabkommen', in: Ludolf Herbst (ed.); Westdeutsch-

land 1945–1955. Unterwerfung, Kontrolle, Integration, Munich: Oldenbourg, 1986, pp. 219–229; Ursula Rombeck-Jaschinski, Das Londoner Schuldenabkommen. Die Regelung der deutschen Auslandsschulden nach dem Zweiten Weltkrieg, Munich: Oldenbourg, 2005.

62 See the reports on SYRIZA's election campaign published in Athens News and Kathimerini Online (English edition) from March 2012 onward, as well as the statements published on SYRIZA's website from February 2012 onward. I want to thank my Greek friends Zissis Papadimitriou and Kostas Lambos for their support in collecting information and analyzing current developments.

63 SYRIZA activists might draw on the concept of "illegitimate debt" they have developed over the past two years, whereby all debts that were created in the context of corrupt machinations or economically senseless military, infrastructural or prestige-oriented projects should be waived.

64 On this and the following, see the reports and statements published on KKE's website from 2009 onward; Communist Party of Greece, 'Theses on Socialism', [http://inter.kke.gr/news/2008news/2008-12-thesis-socialism]; interview with Aleka Papariga, general secretary of the KKE, 8 January 2012, [http://www.kominform.at/article.pap/20120108103943547].

65 Such a mass campaign might agree on the following objectives: a 20-percent reduction in working hours; a 20-percent increase in real wages; the lowering of the legal pension age to 62 years; the slowing down of work rhythms; severance of the link between minimum income and the compulsion to work (a link evident, for instance, in Germany's so-called Hartz IV regulations); introduction of a minimum wage of 1,100 euros; lower unemployment and social insurance contributions; extension of parental leave, care leave and the like (with full compensation).

66 On the systematic correlation between direct democracy and classless societies, see the seminal paper by Kostas Lambos, Amesi dimokratía ke ataxikí konona (Direct Democracy and Classless Society), Thessaloniki 2012.

67 See for example Zissis Papadimitriou, Ston asterismó tis awewaiotitas (Under the Sign of Uncertainty), Thessaloniki 2012.

Contemporary culture has eliminated both the concept of the public and the figure of the intellectual. Former public spaces – both physical and cultural – are now either derelict or colonized by advertising. A cretinous anti-intellectualism presides, cheerled by expensively educated hacks in the pay of multinational corporations who reassure their bored readers that there is no need to rouse themselves from their interpassive stupor. The informal censorship internalized and propagated by the cultural workers of late capitalism generates a banal conformity that the propaganda chiefs of Stalinism could only ever have dreamt of imposing. Zer0 Books knows that another kind of discourse – intellectual without being academic, popular without being populist – is not only possible: it is already flourishing, in the regions beyond the striplit malls of so-called mass media and the neurotically bureaucratic halls of the academy. Zer0 is committed to the idea of publishing as a making public of the intellectual. It is convinced that in the unthinking, blandly consensual culture in which we live, critical and engaged theoretical reflection is more important than ever before.